Mel Bay Presents

Learning Tabla

by David Courtney

CD CONTENTS

3 4 5 6 7 8 9 0

Visit us on the Web at www.melbay.com — E-mail us at email@melbay.com

CONTENTS

 # PREFACE

It is a pleasure to be able to bring you this book. It is a pleasure for several reasons. On one hand I feel very good about being able to make this resource available. The world is a very different place from what it was back in 1972 when I first started to learn tabla. In those days there was no internet and there were no method books for tabla. What little material that was published in India was usually in Hindi and not available at all outside of India. It was very difficult to learn tabla in the West in those days. I resolved that I would do everything that I could so that others would not have as hard of a time as I did. So I am deriving great pleasure in being able to make this material available in an easily obtainable format.

Yet there is another source of my pleasure. It is the extreme pleasure in seeing the tabla become so popular. One cannot turn on the radio, TV, or watch a movie without hearing tabla in the background. Sometimes it is recorded "live" and sometimes it is sampled and played with a MIDI system. Whatever the source, it is a pleasure to know that this instrument has made such a deep impact on our modern global village.

However that is not to say that everything is rosy. Although the internet outlets have made tabla easily available anywhere in the North America and Europe, there is a definite shortage of skilled teachers. Even in the cities where there is a large India population, one often finds that the competent performers are not necessarily competent teachers.

It is for this reason that I am bringing out this book/CD set. In an ideal situation, this set can be used as a teaching tool for a student who already has a good teacher. After all there is no substitute for the human touch. In a less than ideal situation, this set may be used for the student who is hundreds of miles from the nearest teacher. This set may be the only source of instruction. Admittedly this is far from a desirable setup, but one which is the reality for a large number of people. I am considering both of these situations in the layout of this book.

I have tried to keep terminology to a minimum; unfortunately the nature of the subject necessitates a large number of new terms. Every time that a new term is introduced it is explained in depth. Still there are so many new words that it is easy to become overwhelmed. Therefore there is a glossary in the back. Refer to this anytime you encounter a term that you are not familiar with.

I should also explain my use of italics. Formal English dictates that foreign words be italicized. Unfortunately there are so many foreign words in this book that this custom conveys no real information and compromises the layout. Therefore I have adopted the policy of only italicizing the bols (mnemonic syllables) which appear in the text. I feel that this makes for a cleaner layout and enhances readability.

There are a large number of strokes, and "licks". These have corresponding mnemonic syllables. Although they are all explained in detail, their sheer number makes it difficult to keep track. Again there is a list of mnemonic syllables in the back. If you get confused, always check there.

The conclusion of this book also has other things that you may wish to remember. These are such useful bits of information such as where to buy tablas, a bibliography and a few internet sites that you may wish to look at.

As you go through the book you will find that numerous examples have been recorded on the CD. Do refer to the CD to check that your sound is correct.

Please avoid the temptation to play very fast. The prime concern for the new student is not speed, but correct technique and correct sound. Any bad habits you acquire now will be much more difficult to correct later.

Here is one more word of advice. The Roman script does not even do a good job of writing English, so it is hopeless to expect this script to convey the subtitles of the tabla mnemonics. Therefore I have also included the Dev Nagri characters in all of the exercises and compositions. Try to make a habit of looking at these instead of the Roman script and you will avoid a lot of common mistakes.

I just have one final word of advice for the new student. Tabla is one of the most difficult drums in the world. Be patient, study and practice hard. I assure you that if you are truly committed, you will be able to overcome all obstacles and learn this beautiful instrument.

Finally, I must acknowledge several people who have made this book/recording set possible. The first person to thank is my wife Chandrakantha. She played the harmonium, sitar, tanpura, and sang for the audio recording. I would also like to thank Bob Goldman for his input and proofreading.

David Courtney
October 15, 1999

INTRODUCTION

Tabla is the most common drum in India. It is commonly found throughout India, Pakistan, Bangladesh and even into Afghanistan. Since the 1960s it has even been played in The US and Europe. Although it is of Indian origin it is now found around the world.

Indian music is one of the oldest systems of music in the world. It is part of an unbroken musical tradition which extends back about 2000 years. This does not mean that the music has not changed; it has undergone tremendous evolution during this time. What it means is that for the last 2000 years the music has been handed down from teacher to disciple without a break. This system of teacher and disciple is called "Guru-Shishya-Parampara" in Sanskrit.

There are a number of instruments in India. Some of the most famous are the sitar and tabla. Other less well-known instruments are the sarod, sarangi and santur. Many recordings are available of traditional music as well as modern fusion pieces.

There are two systems of classical music in India. There is the North Indian system; this is called Hindustani sangeet. There is also the South Indian system; this is called Carnatic sangeet. The tabla is associated with the North Indian system of music.

There are two aspects of traditional Indian music. There is the melodic form known as "rag", and the rhythmic form known as "tal". Both the rhythmic and the melodic aspects are necessary to move the music along.

The rag is a form that is somewhat similar to the modes of ecclesiastic music, flamenco, or middle eastern music. As in any modal form, concepts such as major scale or minor scale have absolutely no meaning. There are distinctions between the many scales that one would tend to lump together in usual Western terms. Such distinctions take a great amount of study to fully understand.

The word "tal" literally means clap. This is in reference to the Indian system of timekeeping based upon the clapping and waving of the hand. (This will be discussed later.) Just as Western music has a system of baton movements to keep time, it is this system of clapping and waving that lies at the core of Indian timekeeping.

This is just the briefest introduction. It will take a long period of study to fully understand all of these points.

No one knows who invented tabla. No one knows exactly when it was invented. Furthermore, no one knows exactly how it was invented. The only thing that we know for sure is that the tabla showed up on the musical scene about 250 years ago.

There are many legends concerning the invention of the tabla. Let us look at some of the more common ones.

One of the most popular stories has tabla being invented by Amir Khusru (1253-1325). Amir Khusru was a great musician, poet, and saint of the Indian Sufi tradition. He is considered an icon of growing Islamic influence on Indian culture. Although Amir Khusru was certainly a great artist he did not invent the tabla. Amir Khusru lived in the 13th century while the tabla is no more than about 250 years old. Therefore this legend has no basis in fact.

Some suggest that tabla was invented by a disgruntled (or in some stories clumsy) musician who broke his pakhawaj (a barrel shaped drum) in two. It is often said that afterwards he plays the two pieces and exclaims to his delight "tabhi bola!" (It still plays!) Thus the instrument and the term tabla are invented. (Do you really think that this story is plausible? – Yea, right.)

Here is what we know for sure. The word "tabla" is an Arabic word for "drum". Although the Arabic word is generic, the tabla in India is a very specific instrument.

If we are trying to trace the origins of tabla we really have to look at the evolution of three separate things. We need to look at the evolution of the wooden drum, the metal drum, and the music which is played. In the absence of any clearly recorded history we are forced to look to iconography in order to trace the origins of tabla. Looking at paintings and sculptures and checking the dates is a good way to get an idea as to how the tabla developed.

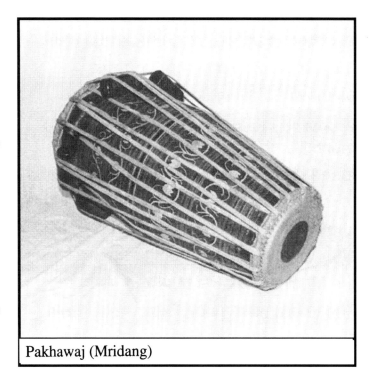

Pakhawaj (Mridang)

The wooden drum appears to have been derived from the pakhawaj or mridanga. Pakhawaj is an ancient instrument. It is a particular form of a class of instruments called mridang. These instruments consist of a barrel shaped body with heads on both sides. They are laced with rawhide. The right hand side is very similar to the tabla, however the left hand side is different. Where the left-hand drum of the tabla has a permanent black spot, the left side of the pakhawaj is plain. It requires a temporary application of flour and water to give a deep resonant sound. After the drum has been played the flour / water mixture must be removed before the drum is put away. The pakhawaj was a popular drum in northern India for many centuries. It is only in the 20th century that it has fallen out of common use.

The metal drum of the tabla seems to have developed differently. The construction of the metal drum, known as "bayan", is very different from the pakhawaj. This indicates that it has a different origin. The construction is very much like the kettle-drums which are found throughout the Middle-East. The most common kettle drum in India today is known as the nagada. Kettle drums appear to have been brought into India by the Muslims several hundred years ago. These drums may be found in different sizes and shapes. They may be played singly, but normally in pairs. Old paintings even show three or more being played at a time.

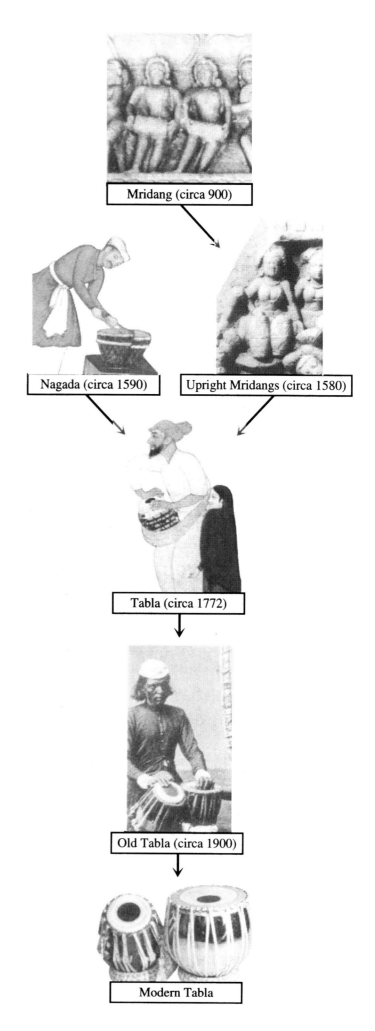

Mridang (circa 900)

Nagada (circa 1590)

Upright Mridangs (circa 1580)

Tabla (circa 1772)

Old Tabla (circa 1900)

Modern Tabla

There are pictures from the 16th century that suggest to us how the tabla may have developed. It appears that pairs of upright mridang were commonly played. At the same time musicians were playing pairs of nagada. At some point someone decided to take one of the upright pakhawajs and one of the kettle drums and play them together. This is really no different from the way that modern percussionists will grab cowbells, cymbals or any of the other percussive instruments and add them to their set.

Now this brings up the next question; where did the music come from? Again we will never know for sure, but it seems that influences came form many sources. The largest contribution appears to be from the pakhawaj. Yet modern performances also show the influences of nagada, dholak (a folk drum) and other instruments.

So this is how the picture emerges. It seems that the tabla, like a Western drumset is an amalgamation of different influences and drums from different places.

For hundreds of years pakhawaj and tabla could both be heard. Tabla was used for women entertainers, known as "tawaif". These functions were usually in smaller chambers where day-to-day activities occurred. On the other hand, the pakhawaj was the instrument used to accompany the men in the royal courts.

The curious effect of having the pakhawaj and tabla used in different situations was profound. The pakhawaj developed a technique that was very loud and powerful while the tabla developed a technique that was delicate. The pakhawaj was loud because there were no sound systems in those days; it was a major challenge to be heard in the large halls. Conversely the tabla was delicate because that was what was appropriate for the accompaniment of women in the smaller chambers. It is the speed and delicacy of the tabla which remains its most alluring feature even today.

In the 18th and 19th centuries numerous stylistic schools known as "gharana" developed. The word gharana literally means "house", and implies the "house of the guru". There are six gharanas and they take their names from the geographical locations where they developed. These gharanas are known as Dilli (Delhi) gharana, Ajrada gharana, Punjab gharana, Benares gharana, Farukhabad gharana, and Lucknow gharana. Each gharana had a different approach to technique, and compositional form.

The later part of the 19th century and early part of the 20th century was a very hard time for the tabla and the tabla players. Many of the music patrons lost their wealth as the political situation in India changed. The British banned the institution of the tawaifs. The term "tabalji" (one who plays the tabla) became a derogatory term evoking connotations of a drunkard or a pimp.

Fortunately things began to look up during the independence movement. There was a reawakening in interest in traditional Indian culture. Performance opportunities increased, and other sources of patronage were established. Today the tabla and its artists are held in higher prestige than they have ever been in the past.

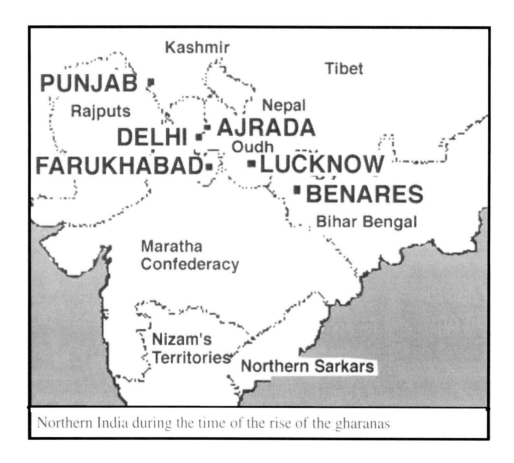

Northern India during the time of the rise of the gharanas

PARTS OF TABLA

Let us familiarize ourselves with the parts of the tabla. In this section we will learn what the parts are, and what they are called. These terms are Hindi and Urdu and are probably the most common. Let us first look at the complete tabla set shown below.

First let us see what is meant by the word "tabla". In common usage the term tabla is applied to both the drums together. Strictly speaking, this not correct. Actually only the smaller wooden drum is the tabla. However the term has been applied to both drums for so many years we will go ahead and bow to common usage. Therefore if we wish to be specific we will call the wooden drum "dayan" and the metal one "bayan".

Let us look at the entire set. First, we have a wooden drum (the dayan); the word dayan means "right". The larger metal drum is called bayan; the word bayan means "left". There are two covers which protect the tabla when not in use, and the two doughnut shaped cushions known as "chutta". There is also a tuning hammer known as "hathodi". We also have to have the talcum powder.

A complete tabla set

Let us look closer at the major parts of the tabla. These parts are the drumhead which is known as "pudi". There is also the rawhide thong (tasma), and the wooden dowels (gatta). There is a wooden shell (lakadi), and a brass shell (pital). There is also the counter hoop which is known as "kundal".

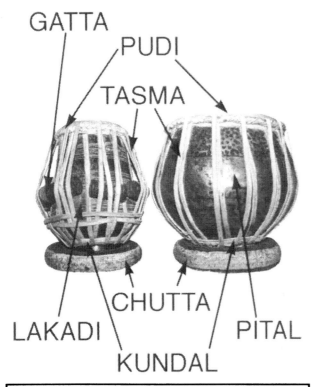

GATTA
PUDI
TASMA
LAKADI
CHUTTA
KUNDAL
PITAL

Parts of the tabla

The pudi (drumhead) has many different parts. The four parts that we need to be concerned with are the black spot (syahi), main membrane (maidan), annular membrane (chat), and the rawhide braid (gajara).

Familiarizing yourself with the parts of the tabla makes many things easier. It allows you to communicate with importers and musicians. It also gives you the necessary background to get started. Obviously these terms simply have to be committed to memory.

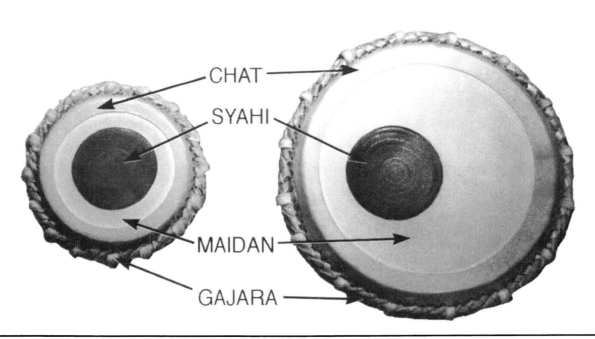

CHAT
SYAHI
MAIDAN
GAJARA

Parts of the pudi

TUNING, CARE & MAINTENANCE

One of the first things we need to know is how to take care of our instrument. Tabla requires some special care.

The most important thing is to keep the black spot (syahi) dry. It is very sensitive to moisture. This is one of the reasons we use talcum powder when we play. Even a small amount of sweat on our hands is enough to damage the tabla. Above all, keep the tabla out of the rain!

Do not play with sticks. If you use wooden drumsticks it will shatter the syahi and force you to replace the entire head. This may sound obvious, but it is amazing how many drums I have seen that were damaged because of this kind of abuse.

Do not expose the tabla to extremes of temperature. Excessive heat may split the skin. Sudden exposure to cold may cause moisture to condense in the syahi and thus ruin it.

Try to keep the tabla in tune. There is a common misconception that a tabla should be loosened whenever it is not going to be played. This is only true when dealing with the poorest quality tablas, such as one might find from Bengal. Doing this for any decent tabla will make it unreliable on stage.

The bayan (metal drum) should be in tune. It is easy to tell if the bayan is in tune once you know how to play, but if you are a novice it is difficult. If the bayan has been sitting in a warehouse for a while, it is highly unlikely that it will be too tight. One then has to decide whether it is correct or too loose. A rule of thumb is that if you can press the center of the bayan and the skin displaces 1/4" before the pressure becomes great, it is probably acceptable. If you can displace the skin in excess of 1/2" inch, it probably needs tightening.

The bayan is tightened by inserting a small gatta under the tasma as shown on the next page. It is easy to make, simply get a wooden dowel with a diameter slightly greater than a common pencil, cut it into approximately 3" lengths and wedge them between the metal shell and the thong. Eight lengths should be enough to raise the drum to the proper pitch. All bayans will need one sooner or later. If your bayan does not have them, by all means put them in.

This fixes the bayan, but what about the dayan?

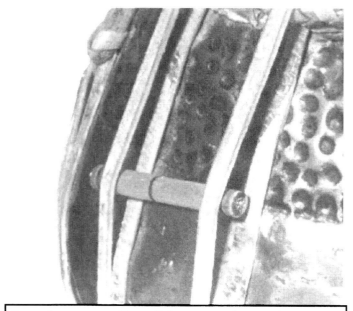

Inserting a gatta (dowel) increases the tension

The dayan (wooden drum) has a stringent requirement for pitch. Tuning is performed on the braid (gajara). One raises the pitch by slightly tightening the skin. This is accomplished by striking down with the hammer (see illustration below). Conversely, one lowers the pitch by slightly loosening the skin. This is accomplished by striking the gajara from the underside. If the gajara does not respond to the hammer, then the wooden dowels (gatta) must be struck. Hammer the wooden dowels down to increase the tension and hammer them up to loosen.

The dayan is tuned up by striking down on the gajara, it is tuned down by up from the underside.

Once the gattas have been moved, return to the gajara for further tuning. We may summarize by saying that the gajara is for fine-tuning while the gatta is for coarse tuning. It is very important that one strikes only the gajara with the hammer. An accidental strike against the wooden lip will irreparably damage the tabla!

When you are trying to tune the tabla-dayan you need to strike the drum so that you will know what you are dealing with. One cannot just strike the drum at random. A rim stroke known as *"Naa"* is a good one to use; this may be learned on page 20. Another useful stroke for tuning is *"Tin"*; this may be learned on page 23.

This still leaves the topic of what pitch to tune to. The table on the next page is a rough guide. Simply measure the pudi across the face of the drum. Do not include the gajara in your measurement. Compare the size of your dayan with the recommended

Tuning the Tabla	
Size of head	Approximate range
4 3/4 inches	C-D♯
5 inches	B-C♯
5 1/4 inches	A♯-D
5 1/2 inches	A-B
5 3/4 inches	F-A
6 inches	E-G

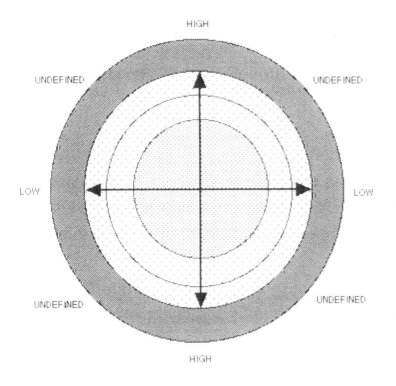

HIGH

UNDEFINED   UNDEFINED

LOW   LOW

UNDEFINED   UNDEFINED

HIGH

An untuned tabla has pitches which form a cross. There are two areas of relatively high pitch opposed by two areas of relatively low pitch.

Listen to track 1 to hear an untuned tabla.

pitch in the table and this will give you a rough idea as to what is an acceptable pitch. I must warn you that this table is just a rough approximation. There are numerous factors about your drumhead which could push your optimum pitch higher or lower.

You may get a digital tuner to help you tune the drum. They are inexpensive and very helpful for the novice. If you are very new to this, you may wish to be cautious and tune to the lower recommended pitch. This will still give an acceptable sound yet lower the chance damaging the dayan.

It is important that the tension around the drum be uniform. A drum which is out-of-tune has a cross pattern of pitches. We see that there are two areas of relatively high pitch and two areas of relatively low pitch. Between them are zones where the pitch is poorly defined. If one is having a hard time hearing the pitch it may be because one is striking an area of undefined pitch. Shift a little around the rim and the pitch is often easier to hear.

The main difficulty in tuning the tabla is due to the difficulty in hearing the pitch. Learning to tune the tabla is just a question of experience.

If we have paid attention to all of the previous points, the tabla is now in tune. We can now turn our attention to learning how to play.

 # SITTING AND POSITIONING THE TABLA

We should now discuss the sitting position and the proper placement of the tabla. Both of which are important first steps to learning how to play.

PLACEMENT OF THE TABLA

First of all the tabla should be placed in the two rings (chutta). These chuttas allow the tabla to resonate freely. The dayan (wooden drum) should be on your right side and the metal drum (bayan) should be on your left. If you are left-handed you should reverse this.

The dayan should be inclined well away from you. This goes against the instinct of the beginner who would like to face it towards you so that you can see it. Facing the dayan away from you is actually a question of ergonomics. This allows the wrists to be kept in a straight position, thus making the playing more efficient and comfortable.

The bayan should be either parallel to the floor or at most only slightly inclined. The syahi (black spot) should be facing away from you, only slightly to your right. Let us rephrase this. If you imagine a face of a clock such that 12 o'clock is pointing exactly opposite you and six o'clock is pointing toward you, the black spot should be located at a 1 o'clock position.

SITTING POSITION

Correct posture is very important. The posture will determine the ease or difficulty that the student will have in controlling the instrument.

Below we see two broadly accepted sitting positions: one for men and the other for women. The man's position is a simple cross-legged position. For the woman's position both legs are to one side and the knees are together. The woman's sitting position is practical if one is wearing a sari, but the sari is being replaced by other styles of clothing. Therefore it is common to see women adopting the cross-legged position of a man.

Two standard positions, one for men and one for women.

The basic cross-legged position is the most common: and for a good reason. In the course of playing, there is a tendency for the tabla to shift out of position. Since the knees are in contact with the drum this gives an added stability. The knees help to keep the drums, especially the bayan, in a proper position.

We should point out that there have been other positions in use over the years, some of which may still be found. For instance one occasionally sees people play while sitting on their knees. This was once a popular position because it avoided the misdemeanor of showing the soles of your feet to the king (this was a definite no-no). Today this style has largely been abandoned due to the discomfort for the tabla player and the inadequate control over the tabla. One also occasionally finds the tabla played with the bayan resting in the lap. This is primarily used by folk musicians. All things considered, it is best to use the standard position.

BASIC EXERCISES

There are a number of strokes that we must master in order to play tabla. In this section we will go over a number of these strokes.

Today there are two overall approaches to technique. Technique is called "baj"; this is a term that you will hear again and again. There is a pure tabla technique which is known as "Dilli baj". It is called this because this style developed in the area of Dilli (Delhi). There is also a technique which shows a heavy influence of pakhawaj. This technique is called "Purbi baj". The word Purbi means "Eastern", and this style is so named because it developed in an area east of Delhi.

Today, musicians are expected to have an understanding of both styles. It is common to mix them together in a single performance. However, when we are learning it is good to start with just one style. When we are comfortable with one, then we can start to learn the other. We will start with the Dilli baj and then move on to learn the Purbi baj. Some teachers may reverse this; it is really just a matter of individual style.

There are two general qualities that characterize the strokes of tabla. The first is a flat, non-resonant stroke traditionally called "band" or closed. The other approach is to have the stroke resonant, known as "khula" or open. However, one must remember that these are just broad categories; each stroke has its own identity that is represented by a "bol".

The "bol" is the Indian system of mnemonics. The term is derived from the Hindi word "bolna" which means, "to speak". In this system, each stroke is assigned a syllable. All permutations are mentally performed on that syllable (bol). The number of strokes and their bols are large, yet only a few are commonly used.

As you move through the material in this section you must recite the bol as you play the exercises. Learning tabla is not like other learning. Learning tabla is more like physical therapy. You are in the process of rewiring your brain. This is a slow and difficult process, so please do not get discouraged. The process of reciting the bol helps to establish the links between the speech processing centers and the parts of the brain that control the motor functions.

There are many subtle variations in pronunciation of the bol. Unfortunately English is poorly equipped to deal with these subtitles. Therefore this book will use a mixed notation. The precise pronunciation and timing is shown in the Dev Nagri script, while a rough English equivalent is shown below it. Try not to use the English; it is most imprecise and will cause you to make unnecessary mistakes. We will also uses a standard rhythmic notation to make the material easier to follow for those of you who are already familiar with it.

Ka (क), **Ke** (के), or **Kin** (किं) - This is a very common stroke. It is also the easiest to execute. One simply strikes the bayan with the flat palm and fingers. Notice that the tips of the fingers extend slightly over the rim. This is a flat slapping sound with no resonance; therefore it is called "band".

Here are some basic exercises using *Ka*:

Exercise 1.　　♩　♩　♩　♩
　　　　　　　　　क　　क　　क　　क
　　　　　　　　　Ka　Ka　Ka　Ka

Ka (a simple slap)

In this exercise we are playing one *Ka* per beat. Notice that in the traditional notation we merely have to write down the bol and the rhythm is presumed to be one stroke per beat.

In Indian music the beat is known as a "matra". Therefore the last exercise was four matras.

Here is another exercise:

Exercise 2.　　♩　　　　♩　♩
　　　　　　　　　क　　 -　　क　　क
　　　　　　　　　Ka　　　Ka　Ka

Listen to track 2 to hear Exercise #1

Listen to track 3 to hear Exercise #2

This last exercise introduces us to the rest or an elongation. In this case, the rest is only one beat. Since the tabla makes no distinction between a rest and an elongated note, we could express the rhythm of the last exercise simply as: half-note, quarter-note, quarter-note.

It is actually easier to think of the last exercise in traditional Indian terms than it is to translate it into Western concepts. In traditional terms we see that the first *Ka* is held over to the second matra. This is designated by the dash. Again in traditional tabla notation there is no difference between an elongation and a rest.

Here is another exercise:

Exercise 3.   ♩ ♩ ♩ ♫

क   क   क   क क
Ka   Ka   Ka   Ka Ka

Listen to track 4 to hear
Exercise #3

This last exercise introduces us to the concept of fractions of matras (e.g., eight-note, sixteenth notes, etc.). The last matra contains two *Kas*, therefore each *Ka* is only half a matra in length.

Remember not to place an unnecessary rest at the end of this exercise. The interval between the two half-matra *Kas* is the same as the interval between the last *Ka* and the first *Ka* of the next cycle. This should be clear from listening to the recording.

Listen to track 5 to hear
Exercise #4

Exercise 4.   ♩   ♫   ♩   ♫

क   क क   क   क क
Ka   Ka Ka   Ka   Ka Ka

I do not think that this exercise needs any further explanation. It is based upon the same principals that were shown in the earlier exercises. By now you see how it all works.

Naa (ना) - This is a common stroke of the right hand. It is produced by holding the last two fingers lightly against the edge of the syahi and using the index finger to forcefully hit the rim (chat) of the tabla. It is important to keep the middle finger extended so as not to hit the drum.

Naa comes in two flavors. One style keeps the finger in constant contact with the drum. The other one allows the finger to bounce off. Experiment with both styles to see the slight difference in tone. For the rest of this book we recommend keeping the finger down.

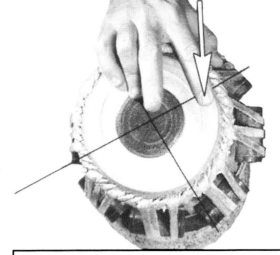

Naa, or Taa (a rim stroke)

Naa is especially important because it forces us to develop the concept of a "home position". This is the position our hand assumes which will allow us to make the maximum variety of strokes. It is also to this position we will always try to return. This home position is based upon an "X" which crosses the drum. This "X" has one line which extends from the ring finger, through the center and bisects the drum. The other line runs from the center at 90° from the first line. It is upon this line that most of the resonant strokes (i.e., khula) are made. This is shown in the previous illustration. This "X" is not merely a conceptual tool but is an actual reflection of the physics of tabla resonance.

Exercise 5.

ना   ना   ना   ना
Naa   Naa   Naa   Naa

Exercise 6.

ना   -   ना   ना
Naa   Naa   Naa

Exercise 7.

ना   ना   ना   ना ना
Naa   Naa   Naa   NaaNaa

Exercise 8.

ना   ना ना   ना   ना ना
Naa   NaaNaa   Naa   NaaNaa

Exercise 9.

ना   क   ना   क
Naa   Ka   Naa   Ka

Listen to the recording for the following exercise:

track 6 - ex #5
track 7 - ex #6
track 8 - ex #7
track 9 - ex #8
track 10 - ex #9

Ga (ग) **Ge** (गे) or **Gin** (गिं) - This is a stroke of the left hand. It is produced by holding the wrist down and arching the fingers over the syahi. The middle and ring-fingers then strike the maidan (the exposed skin between the syahi and the chat.) One must always remember that this is khula or open stroke, therefore it must be very resonant.

Ga, Ge or Gin (open stroke)

21

Ga may be difficult for the beginner. There is a tendency to strike the drum and withdraw the hand under conscious control. Such action cannot be performed consciously. It is essential that the fingers and hand be relaxed the instant the drum is struck so that the hand can rebound of its own accord; like a ricochet. Only then can you hear the full open sound that characterizes this stroke.

Ga is also important because it is the "home position" for the left hand. My guru used to say that the position of the hand should be as a cobra poised to attack.

Exercise 10.

ग　　ग　　ग　　ग
Ga　Ga　Ga　Ga

Exercise 11.

ग　　-　　ग　　ग
Ga　　　　Ga　Ga

Exercise 12.

ग　　ग　　ग　　ग ग
Ga　Ga　Ga　Ga Ga

Exercise 13.

ग　　ग ग　　ग　　ग ग
Ga　Ga Ga　Ga　Ga Ga

> Listen to the recording for the following exercise:
>
> track 11 - ex #10
> track 12 - ex #11
> track 13 - ex #12
> track 14 - ex #13
> track 15 - ex #14

Taa (ता) - The Dilli approach to *Taa* is to play it exactly like *Naa* (pg. 20).

Exercise 14.

ता　　ता　　ता　　ता
Taa　Taa　Taa　Taa

Dhaa (धा) - This is a bol that uses both hands. It is a combination of *Taa (Naa)* and *Ga.*

Dhaa is played by playing Naa (Taa) and Ga simultaneously.

Here are some exercises using this bol:

Exercise 15.   ♩   ♩   ♩   ♩

धा   धा   धा   धा
Dhaa Dhaa Dhaa Dhaa

Exercise 16.   ♩   ♩   ♩

धा   -   धा   धा
Dhaa   Dhaa Dhaa

Exercise 17.   ♩   ♩   ♩   ♫

धा   धा   धा   धा धा
Dhaa Dhaa Dhaa DhaaDhaa

Exercise 18.   ♩   ♫   ♩   ♫

धा   धा धा   धा   धा धा
Dhaa DhaaDhaa Dhaa DhaaDhaa

Listen to the recording for the following exercise:

track 16 - ex #15
track 17 - ex #16
track 18 - ex #17
track 19 - ex #18

Tin (तिं) - This stroke is made with the right hand. Its hand position is very similar to *Naa*; yet, it is much softer and more delicate. This stroke is produced by placing the last two fingers of the right hand lightly against the syahi and striking on the border between the syahi and the maidan. Our "X" pattern is again used for this stroke. As with *Naa*, the middle finger is extended and does not strike the drum. Great care must be taken so that the stroke is resonant. This resonance will only come if it is a light ricochet. The exact striking position is determined by the construction of the drum but it is usually at the border of the syahi and maidan. Beginners often have a difficult time making *Tin* sound different from *Taa*. There are two points to keep in mind; first, the stroke must be resonant; second, it must be played very softly.

Tin is a resonant stroke of the right hand.

23

Here are some exercises using Tin.

Exercise 19.

♩ ♩ ♩ ♩

तिं तिं तिं तिं
Tin Tin Tin Tin

Exercise 20.

𝅗𝅥 ♩ ♩

तिं - तिं तिं
Tin   Tin Tin

Exercise 21.

♩ ♩ ♩ ♫

तिं तिं तिं तिं तिं
Tin Tin Tin Tin Tin

Exercise 22.

♩ ♫ ♩ ♫

तिं तिं तिं तिं तिं तिं
Tin Tin Tin Tin Tin Tin

Exercise 23.

𝅗𝅥 ♩ ♩

तिं - ना ना
Tin   Naa Naa

Listen to the recording for the following exercise:

track 20 - ex #19
track 21 - ex #20
track 22 - ex #21
track 23 - ex #22
track 24 - ex #23
track 25 - ex #24
track 26 - ex #25
track 27 - ex #26

Dhin (धिं) - This stroke is the simultaneous playing of *Tin* and *Ga*. We must remember to keep the right hand very soft.

Here are some exercises:

Exercise 24.

♩ ♩ ♩ ♩

धिं धिं धिं धिं
Dhin Dhin Dhin Dhin

Exercise 25.

𝅗𝅥 ♩ ♩

धिं - धिं धिं
Dhin   Dhin Dhin

Exercise 26.

𝅗𝅥 ♩ ♩

धिं - ना ना
Dhin   Naa Naa

Dhin is made by playing Tin and Ga simultaneously.

TAL AND THEKA

Tal and theka are very important to the tabla player. The concept of tal may be roughly equated to a rhythmic concept, while theka may be translated to mean a specific "groove". If we wish to use a Western analogy we could say that the tal would be a basic concept such as "common time". Theka on the other hand is analogous to a specific beat, for example a basic "rock" beat.

TAL

As mentioned earlier the word "tal" indicates the basic rhythmic concept. The word "tal" itself means "the clapping of hands". The clapping of hands is the most basic form of timekeeping imaginable. Tal is based upon three different levels of structure; the beat, the measure, and the cycle.

The beat in Indian music is conceptually the same as it is in Western music. In India it is called "matra". As in Western music, the duration of the beat is short in fast tempos, conversely it is long in slow pieces.

There is also a measure in Indian music; it is called "vibhag". The concept of the measure and the vibhag are the same except for some small differences. The most important difference is that the vibhag is not given much importance. This is because the majority of Indian music is performed in what we would call mixed measure. That is to say measures of two, three, or four beats are commonly mixed together. We will see that this mix is not random but is carefully prescribed by the structure of the tal.

There is another interesting characteristic of the vibhag; this characteristic is linked to the system of timekeeping. Indian timekeeping is based upon a system of claps and waves of the hand. Every vibhag (measure) must be assigned either a clap or a wave. This system of clapping and waving is somewhat analogous to the movements of the conductor's baton. The clap is known as "tali" and the wave is known as "khali". This formalized system allows for effective communication on stage without having to stop a performance.

The third element of our tal is the cycle; this is known as "avartan". The cycle is somewhat analogous to the cycle in Western music (e.g., 16 bar blues pattern). There are however fundamental differences. The most important difference is the level of significance. In Western music the cycle is a mere convenience that may be broken when it is artistically desired. On the other hand the cycle in Indian music is considered inviolate. One must not break the cycle under any circumstances.

THEKA

Theka may be thought of as a "groove". It is a basic pattern of bols used to accompany the music. However the theka has become more than a mere accompaniment; over the last 200 years it has emerged to become the defining feature of the tal. We will now look at a few common examples.

We will start by presenting some counting exercises. Count these exercises out aloud and clap along with them. This will make the abstract forms of the tal clear. We will give two counting exercises, one to emphasize the vibhag (measure) and another to emphasize the avartan (cycle).

There are four exercises for each tal. The first two are the counting exercises. Next, one recites and claps the bols of the theka, finally one plays and recites the theka. In the accompanying recording the vocalization of the bol will not be continuous. This is simply so that you can have a clearly recorded reference as to what the tabla is supposed to sound like. You should **ALWAYS** recite the bol while practicing.

There are a few more points on the notation that we should keep in mind. Notice that the beginning of each vibhag is denoted with a small symbol. These symbols denote the clapping and waving patterns. First notice the "0" at the start of the third vibhag. This denotes a wave of the hand (khali). The numbers "2" and "3", denote the second clap and third clap respectively. Notice that there is no "1", but that it has been replaced by an "X", (sometimes you will find "+"). The use of these symbols is an indication that the beginning of each cycle is special, it is called "sam" (pronounced as "sum" as in "summation"). We will see later on that the sam has a special significance for the performance of Indian music.

Tintal - 16 matras (4+4+4+4) - Many people consider this tal to be the oldest and most fundamental rhythm in north India. Tintal consists of four vibhags of four matras each. The defining pattern of clapping is: clap, clap, wave, clap. It is used in classical forms of music.

Tintal Counting Exercise #1

^{x}1	2	3	4		^{2}1	2	3	4	
^{o}1	2	3	4		^{3}1	2	3	4	

Tintal Counting Exercise #2

^{x}1	2	3	4		^{2}5	6	7	8	
^{o}9	10	11	12		^{3}13	14	15	16	

Listen to track 28
to hear Tintal

Theka

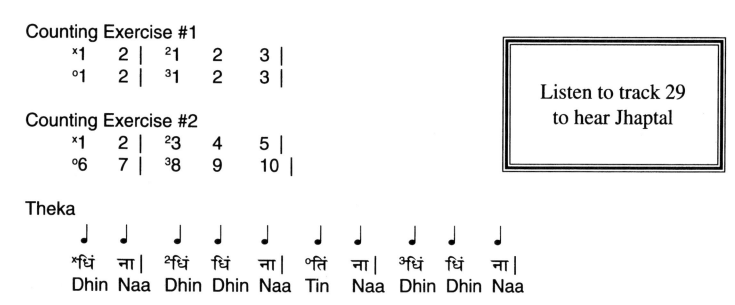

ˣधा	धिं	धिं	धा		²धा	धिं	धिं	धा	
Dhaa	Dhin	Dhin	Dhaa	Dhaa	Dhin	Dhin	Dhaa
°धा	तिं	तिं	ना		³ना	धिं	धिं	धा	
Dhaa	Tin	Tin	Naa	Naa	Dhin	Dhin	Dhaa

Jhaptal - 10 matras (2+3+2+3) This tal consists of 10 matras of four vibhags. It is divided into two matras, three matras, two matras, and three matras. It is designated clap, clap, wave, clap. Jhaptal is used in both classical as well as semiclassical Indian music.

Counting Exercise #1

ˣ1　2 | ²1　2　3 |
°1　2 | ³1　2　3 |

Counting Exercise #2

ˣ1　2 | ²3　4　5 |
°6　7 | ³8　9　10 |

Listen to track 29
to hear Jhaptal

Theka

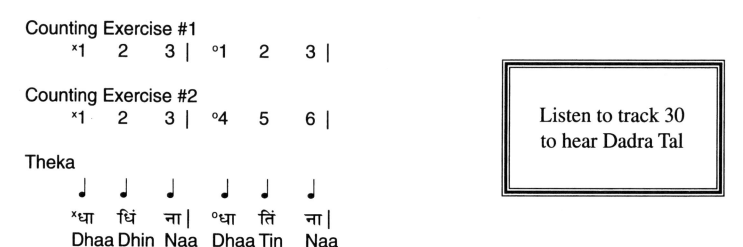

ˣधिं	ना		²धिं	धिं	ना		°तिं	ना		³धिं	धिं	ना	
Dhin	Naa	Dhin	Dhin	Naa	Tin	Naa	Dhin	Dhin	Naa

Dadra - 6 matras (3+3) This tal is compose of 6 matras, divided into two vibhags of three matras each. It is simply designated by: clap, wave. It is commonly used in the lighter styles of music.

Counting Exercise #1

ˣ1　2　3 | °1　2　3 |

Counting Exercise #2

ˣ1　2　3 | °4　5　6 |

Listen to track 30
to hear Dadra Tal

Theka

ˣधा	धिं	ना		°धा	तिं	ना	
Dhaa	Dhin	Naa	Dhaa	Tin	Naa

Dipchandi - 14 matras (3+4+3+4) Dipchandi is composed of four vibhags. These vibhags are three matras, four matras, three matras, and four matras respectively. It is designated by: clap, clap, wave, clap. Dipchandi is commonly used in semiclassical Indian music.

Counting Exercise #1

^{x}1   2   3 | ^{2}1   2   3   4 |
^{o}1   2   3 | ^{3}1   2   3   4 |

Counting Exercise #2

^{x}1   2   3 | ^{2}4   5   6   7 |
^{o}8   9   10 | ^{3}11   12   13   14 |

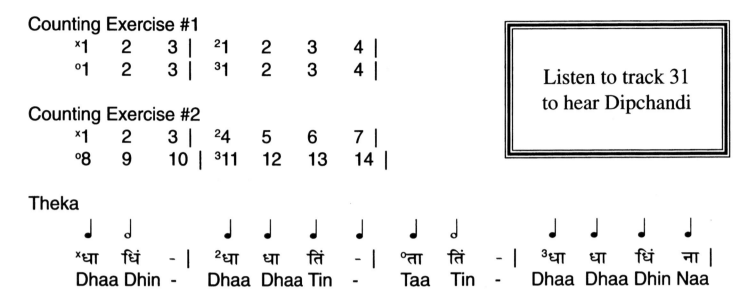

Listen to track 31 to hear Dipchandi

Theka

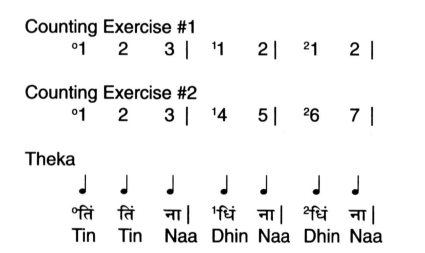

^{x}धा धिं - | ^{2}धा धा तिं - | ^{o}ता तिं - | ^{3}धा धा धिं ना |
Dhaa Dhin -   Dhaa Dhaa Tin -   Taa Tin -   Dhaa Dhaa Dhin Naa

Rupak Tal - 7 matras (3+2+2) Rupak tal is composed of seven matras. It is divided into three vibhags of three matras, two matras, and two matras respectively. It is designated by a wave, clap, clap. Rupak is unique among all of the Indian tals in that the sam is khali, that is to say that there is a wave of the hands on the first beat. Rupak tal is used in classical, semiclassical and even in lighter forms of music.

Counting Exercise #1

^{o}1   2   3 | ^{1}1   2 | ^{2}1   2 |

Counting Exercise #2

^{o}1   2   3 | ^{1}4   5 | ^{2}6   7 |

Listen to track 32 to hear Rupak

Theka

^{o}तिं तिं ना | ^{1}धिं ना | ^{2}धिं ना |
Tin   Tin   Naa Dhin Naa Dhin Naa

28

MODULATION

Modulation is the act of bending the pitch of the bayan. This is one of the tabla's most distinctive sounds and is a technique that we must master if we are going to make our playing expressive. In its simplest, modulation is nothing more than the application of pressure with the wrist. However, in practice, it is a very difficult art to master, one which may take many years.

There are a few more techniques that we will have to learn. These techniques are linked to our ability to make modulations.

1-finger Ga

Here is another way to play *Ga*. It is conceptually identical to the two-finger *Ga* shown earlier except only the index finger strikes. Since the one-finger *Ga* is inherently weaker than a two-finger *Ga*, it should only be used whenever speed is required.

Here are a few exercises that we can use to obtain speed. Later we will see how they are used in our modulations.

Listen to track 33
to hear Exercise #27

Exercise 27.

♩	♩	♩	♩
ग	ग	ग	ग
Ga	Ga	Ga	Ga
2 finger	1 finger	2 finger	1 finger

Throughout the rest of this book whenever we wish to specify a one or two -finger *Ga* we will simply put a "1" or a "2" underneath. (Normally we will not specify it. After a certain point we feel that each individual has the artistic maturity to make their own decisions about technique.) Therefore the upper exercise may be rewritten as:

♩	♩	♩	♩
ग	ग	ग	ग
Ga	Ga	Ga	Ga
2	1	2	1

Let us return to the topic of modulation. Modulation is the process of bending the pitch on the bayan. It is very expressive and is perhaps the tabla's most impressive sound. It is executed by a myriad of changes in position and pressure.

Here is an exercise with only our two-finger *Ga*. In this exercise all of the *Ga*s. are exactly like we have been playing them earlier except the first. This *Ga* we will play by sliding our wrist forward into the bayan, applying a considerable amount of pressure and then striking with our two-fingers.

Exercise 28.

♩	♩	♩	♩
ग	ग	ग	ग
Ga	Ga	Ga	Ga
2- press	2	2	2

Let us now try the same exercise but this time use our one-finger *Ga*.

Exercise 29.

♩	♩	♩	♩
ग	ग	ग	ग
Ga	Ga	Ga	Ga
1- press	2	1	2

Here are a few more exercises for us:

Exercise 30.

♩	♩	♩	♩
ग	ग	ग	ग
Ga	Ga	Ga	Ga
2- press	1	2- press	1

Exercise 31.

♩	♩	♩	♩
ग	ग	ग	ग
Ga	Ga	Ga	Ga
2	1-press	2	1-press

Listen to the recording for the following exercise:

track 34 - ex #28
track 35 - ex #29
track 36 - ex #30
track 37 - ex #31

Do not be confused if these exercises sound similar; this is the entire purpose. We wish to have several techniques to produce the same sound. These options will come in useful later when we wish to build up our speed.

There is another type of modulation which is characterized by a "whooping" sound. This particular modulation is especially useful in the folk and filmi styles. This is similar to the "forward-press" that we have been playing except for one important difference. In the last "forward-press" we would shift forward, press, and then strike the drum. To get our "whoop", we strike the drum at the same time that we are sliding forward and pressing. Here are some exercises based upon this modulation.

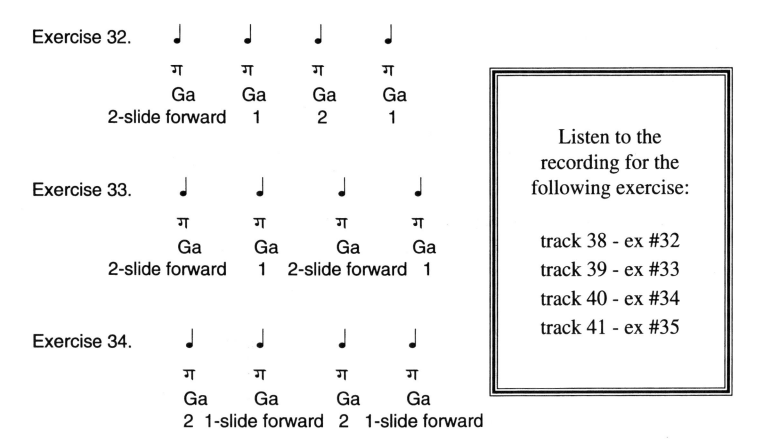

Exercise 32.

ग ग ग ग
Ga Ga Ga Ga
2-slide forward 1 2 1

Exercise 33.

ग ग ग ग
Ga Ga Ga Ga
2-slide forward 1 2-slide forward 1

Exercise 34.

ग ग ग ग
Ga Ga Ga Ga
2 1-slide forward 2 1-slide forward

Listen to the recording for the following exercise:

track 38 - ex #32
track 39 - ex #33
track 40 - ex #34
track 41 - ex #35

There is a third type of modulation which is quite common. This is a reverse slide. For this, one simple places the wrist forward on the bayan touching the syahi, and applying considerable pressure, then strike. Concurrent to this strike one slides the hand back to our home position (i.e. toward the body). While one is sliding the pressure should be released. This modulation is very much used within the classical styles. It has a rich and somber feel but is unfortunately quite difficult. Even though it is quite difficult it is one which must be mastered. Here are some exercises:

Exercise 35.

ग ग ग ग
Ga Ga Ga Ga
2-slide back 2-slide back 2-slide back 2-slide back

There is one more modulation which we will deal with in this chapter; this is the combined technique. It has a rich and mellow sound and is very popular with the audiences. The first half of this combination is exactly like our reverse slide. The twist comes at the instant we reach our home position; at this point we must slide forward and increases the pressure; but we do not re-strike the drum. If this stroke is executed correctly we can slide backwards, then forwards without loosing the sound. Here are some exercises:

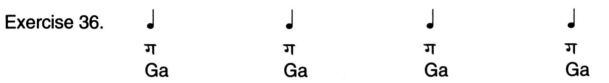

Exercise 36.

               ग   ग   ग   ग
              Ga   Ga   Ga   Ga

2-slide back/forward   2-slide back/forward 2-slide back/forward 2-slide back/forward

We have spent a considerable amount of time working on our left hand. If these exercises are mastered we will make excellent progress toward making our playing more musical and expressive.

Listen to track 42
to hear Ex. #36

MORE BOLS

Let us now learn some more bols. These bols will allow us to progress in our studies.

BOL EXPRESSIONS

The "bol complex" or "bol expression" is a large phrase composed of multiple syllables. Do not try to break these complex expressions down. If you do, then you will just get confused. Let us resort to an analogy for this point. The expression "baseball stadium" is a single concept. This expression could be broken down into three words "base", "ball", and "stadium". But we can see that the concept of the word "ball" is a very different concept from a "baseball stadium". As we move through this section the nature of these warnings will become clear.

Ti Ta (ति ट) - *TiTa* is an example of a bol expression made of two strokes. There are several techniques for executing this stroke, but we shall describe only the Dilli approach in this section. *Ti* is made by striking the center of the syahi with the middle finger. This is a non-resonant (bandh) stroke. *Ta* is made by striking the center of the syahi with the index finger. This too is a non-resonant (bandh) stroke and should have a sound that is indistinguishable from *Ti*.

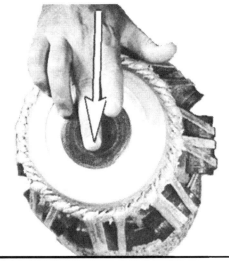 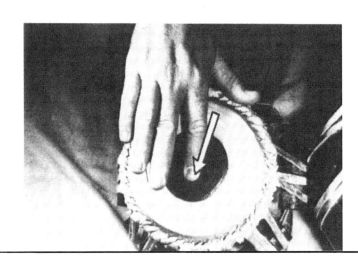

Dilli style TiTa

Here are some exercises:

Exercise 37.

♩	♩	♩	♩
ति	ट	ति	ट
Ti	Ta	Ti	Ta

Listen to track 43 to hear Ex. #37

Exercise 38.

♩   ♩   ♩

धा - ति ट

Dhaa   Ti   Ta

Exercise 39.

♩   ♩   ♩

धा ति ट -

Dhaa Ti   Ta

Listen to the recording for the following exercise:

track 44 - ex #38
track 45 - ex #39

Ti Ra Ki Ta (ति र कि ट) - This bol is composed of four strokes. There are two basic techniques: one Dilli and one Purbi (we have not discussed the Purbi style yet). Additionally there are numerous combination techniques. Again we will describe the Dilli style. The technique is a little bit more complicated than our *TiTa*. The *Ti* is played with the middle-finger of the right hand against the syahi. The *Ra* is played with the index-finger of the right hand against the syahi. The *Ki* is played with the flat left hand. *Ta* is played with the last two fingers of the right hand against the edge of the syahi. These strokes are played in a non-resonant fashion (bandh) and should have equal loudness.

Dilli style Ti for TiRaKiTa

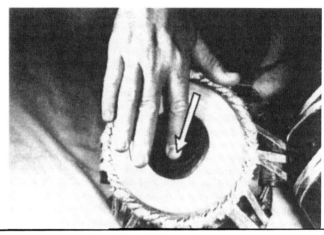

Dilli style Ra for TiRaKiTa

Ki for TiRaKiTa

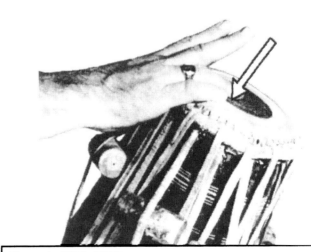

Ta as in TiRaKiTa

Here are some exercises:

Exercise 40. ♩ ♩ ♩ ♩

ति   र   कि   ट
Ti   Ra   Ki   Ta

Exercise 41. ♩ ♩ ♫ ♫

धा   धा   तिर   किट
Dhaa Dhaa Ti Ra Ki Ta

Listen to the recording for the following exercise:

track 46 - ex #40
track 47 - ex #41

Tee (ती) - This bol is made by striking the center of the syahi with the middle finger of the right hand. It is nothing more than the first part of *TiTa*.

Here are some exercises:

Exercise 42. ♩ ♩ ♩ ♩

धा   ती   धा   ती
Dhaa Tee Dhaa Tee

Exercise 43. ♩ ♩ ♩ ♩

धा   ती   धा   ना
Dhaa Tee Dhaa Naa

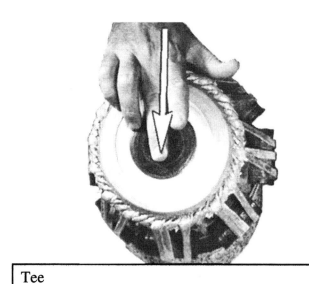

Tee

There is another interpretation of *Tee*. This way is to consider *Tee* to be synonymous with *Tin*. The context will usually tell you which of these two forms is indicated.

Too (तू) - This is a resonant stroke (khula) of the right hand. The head is struck in the center of the syahi with the index finger of the right hand and is not muted at all.

Listen to the recording for the following exercise:

track 48 - ex #42
track 49 - ex #43

Here are some exercises:

Listen to the recording for the following exercise:

track 50 - ex #44
track 51 - ex #45

Exercise 44.

♩   ♩   ♩   ♩

धा   ना   तृ   ना

Dhaa Naa Too Naa

Exercise 45.

♩   ♩   ♩   ♩

धा   तृ   ना   ना

Dhaa Too Naa Naa

Toon (तूं) This is nothing more than another way of saying *Too* (तृ).

Kat (कत्) - This bol may be played several ways. It is always a flat sound, but it can be made either with the left or right hand. You must look at the particular context to determine the correct fingering. In many cases *Kat* is simply another bol for a standard *Ka*. However the position is usually a little different. One usually brings the hand back. A relatively rare form of *Kat* is to play it with the right hand.

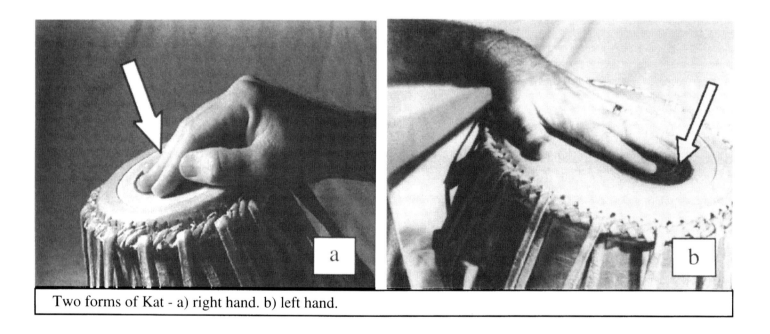

Two forms of Kat - a) right hand. b) left hand.

Dhee (धी) - This bol may be played any of several ways. As a simple, single bol it is generally considered synonymous with *Dhin*. There are two common techniques. One technique is to simultaneously play *Tin* and *Ga* (pg. 24). However an alternate technique is to play *Too* and *Ga* simultaneously.

Kra (क्र) or (क्र) - *Kra* is a flam which is made by first striking the drum with the left hand in a non-resonant fashion (i.e., *Ka*) and then almost, but not quite at the same time coming down with our last two fingers of the right hand.

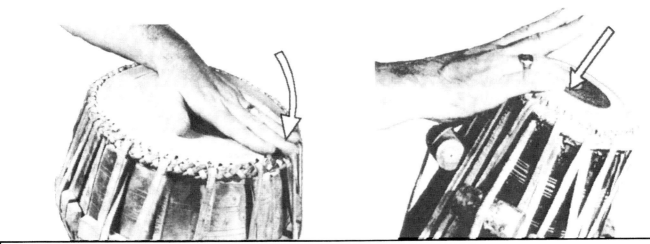

Kra - This is a flam made by first playing the left hand, then the right.

Here is an exercise to become comfortable with Kra.

Exercise 46

धा   -   -   क्र
Dhaa   -   -   Kra

Listen to track 52
to hear Ex. #46

KAIDA

The kaida is a form of theme and variation. The word "kaida" literally means "A system of rules". The musical kaida may be thought of as a system of formulae by which we generate theme and variations.

Kaida is useful to the student for two reasons. First, it gives the student practice in the commonly used patterns of bols; second, it is an introduction to the tabla solo. These kaidas must be committed to memory.

KAIDA #1

Here is a beginner's kaida:

Theka

×धा	धिं	धिं	धा |
Dhaa	Dhin	Dhin	Dhaa

²धा	धिं	धिं	धा |
Dhaa	Dhin	Dhin	Dhaa

⁰धा	तिं	तिं	ना |
Dhaa	Tin	Tin	Naa

³ना	धिं	धिं	धा |
Naa	Dhin	Dhin	Dhaa

> Listen to track 53
> to hear Kaida #1

Kaida (theme) Introduction

धा	धा	ति	ट	धा	धा	तू	ना
Dhaa	Dhaa	Ti	Ta	Dhaa	Dhaa	Too	Naa

ता	ता	ति	ट	धा	धा	धिं	ना
Taa	Taa	Ti	Ta	Dhaa	Dhaa	Dhin	Naa

38

Full speed

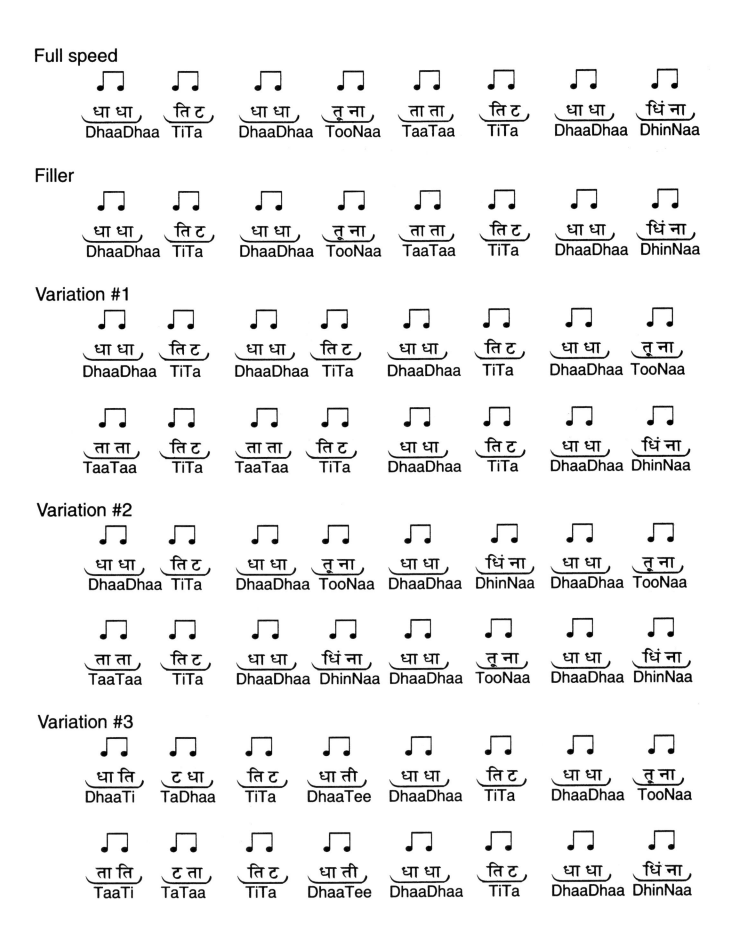

धा धा	ति ट	धा धा	तु ना	ता ता	ति ट	धा धा	धिं ना
DhaaDhaa	TiTa	DhaaDhaa	TooNaa	TaaTaa	TiTa	DhaaDhaa	DhinNaa

Filler

धा धा	ति ट	धा धा	तु ना	ता ता	ति ट	धा धा	धिं ना
DhaaDhaa	TiTa	DhaaDhaa	TooNaa	TaaTaa	TiTa	DhaaDhaa	DhinNaa

Variation #1

धा धा	ति ट	धा धा	ति ट	धा धा	ति ट	धा धा	तु ना
DhaaDhaa	TiTa	DhaaDhaa	TiTa	DhaaDhaa	TiTa	DhaaDhaa	TooNaa

ता ता	ति ट	ता ता	ति ट	धा धा	ति ट	धा धा	धिं ना
TaaTaa	TiTa	TaaTaa	TiTa	DhaaDhaa	TiTa	DhaaDhaa	DhinNaa

Variation #2

धा धा	ति ट	धा धा	तु ना	धा धा	धिं ना	धा धा	तु ना
DhaaDhaa	TiTa	DhaaDhaa	TooNaa	DhaaDhaa	DhinNaa	DhaaDhaa	TooNaa

ता ता	ति ट	धा धा	धिं ना	धा धा	तु ना	धा धा	धिं ना
TaaTaa	TiTa	DhaaDhaa	DhinNaa	DhaaDhaa	TooNaa	DhaaDhaa	DhinNaa

Variation #3

धा ति	ट धा	ति ट	धा ती	धा धा	ति ट	धा धा	तु ना
DhaaTi	TaDhaa	TiTa	DhaaTee	DhaaDhaa	TiTa	DhaaDhaa	TooNaa

ता ति	ट ता	ति ट	धा ती	धा धा	ति ट	धा धा	धिं ना
TaaTi	TaTaa	TiTa	DhaaTee	DhaaDhaa	TiTa	DhaaDhaa	DhinNaa

Tihai (ending cadenza)

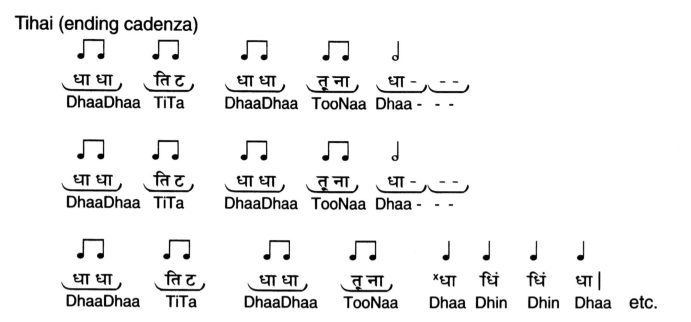

धा धा ‿ ति ट ‿ धा धा ‿ तु ना ‿ धा - ‿ - -
DhaaDhaa TiTa DhaaDhaa TooNaa Dhaa - - -

धा धा ‿ ति ट ‿ धा धा ‿ तु ना ‿ धा - ‿ - -
DhaaDhaa TiTa DhaaDhaa TooNaa Dhaa - - -

धा धा ‿ ति ट ‿ धा धा ‿ तु ना ‿ ˣधा धिं धिं धा |
DhaaDhaa TiTa DhaaDhaa TooNaa Dhaa Dhin Dhin Dhaa   etc.

The technique seems to be self explanatory except for the *Tee* in variation #3. In our earlier discussion of the bol *Tee*, we indicated that it had several interpretations. Within the context of this kaida we must play it by using the middle finger in the center of the syahi in a nonresonant fashion. We know this because the *Tee* here is obviously derived from the bol *TiTa*. Therefore the same technique that we used for the *Ti* we now use for the *Tee*.

KAIDA #2
Theka

ˣधा धिं धिं धा |
Dhaa Dhin Dhin Dhaa

²धा धिं धिं धा |
Dhaa Dhin Dhin Dhaa

°धा तिं तिं ना |
Dhaa Tin Tin Naa

ˣना धिं धिं धा |
Naa Dhin Dhin Dhaa

> Listen to track 54
> to hear Kaida #2

40

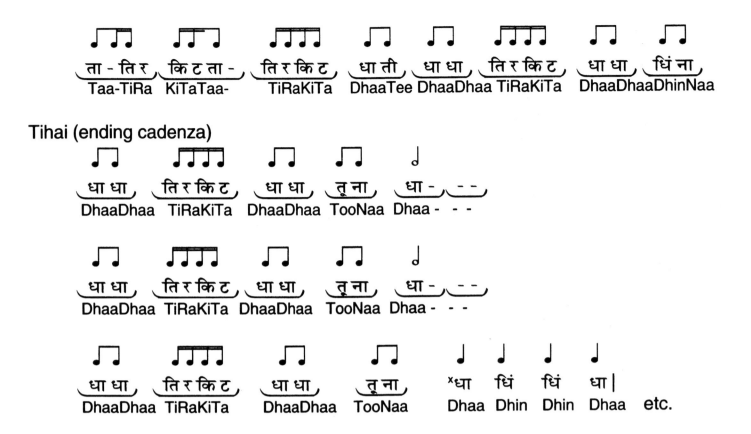

ता - तिर किट ता - तिर किट, धा ती धा धा तिर किट, धा धा धिं ना
Taa-TiRa KiTaTaa- TiRaKiTa DhaaTee DhaaDhaa TiRaKiTa DhaaDhaaDhinNaa

Tihai (ending cadenza)

धा धा, तिर किट, धा धा, तू ना, धा - - -
DhaaDhaa TiRaKiTa DhaaDhaa TooNaa Dhaa - - -

धा धा, तिर किट, धा धा, तू ना, धा - - -
DhaaDhaa TiRaKiTa DhaaDhaa TooNaa Dhaa - - -

धा धा, तिर किट, धा धा, तू ना, ×धा धिं धिं धा |
DhaaDhaa TiRaKiTa DhaaDhaa TooNaa Dhaa Dhin Dhin Dhaa etc.

KAIDA #3

Here is another kaida.

Theka

×धा धिं धिं धा |
Dhaa Dhin Dhin Dhaa

²धा धिं धिं धा |
Dhaa Dhin Dhin Dhaa

°धा तिं तिं ना |
Dhaa Tin Tin Naa

³ना धिं धिं धा |
Naa Dhin Dhin Dhaa

Listen to track 55
to hear Kaida #3

Theme

धा	ती	धा	ती	धा	धा	तिर	किट
Dhaa	Tee	Dhaa	Tee	Dhaa	Dhaa	Ti Ra	Ki Ta

धा	ती	धा	ती	धा	धा	तू	ना
Dhaa	Tee	Dhaa	Tee	Dhaa	Dhaa	Too	Naa

ता	ती	ता	ती	ता	ता	तिर	किट
Taa	Tee	Taa	Tee	Taa	Taa	Ti Ra	Ki Ta

धा	ती	धा	ती	धा	धा	धिं	ना
Dhaa	Tee	Dhaa	Tee	Dhaa	Dhaa	Dhin	Naa

Full Speed

धा ती	धा ती	धा धा	तिर किट
DhaaTee	DhaaTee	DhaaDhaa	TiRaKiTa

धा ती	धा ती	धा धा	तू ना
DhaaTee	DhaaTee	DhaaDhaa	TooNaa

ता ती	ता ती	ता ता	तिर किट
TaaTee	TaaTee	TaaTaa	TiRaKiTa

धा ती	धा ती	धा धा	धिं ना
DhaaTee	DhaaTee	DhaaDhaa	DhinNaa

Second Iteration

धा ती	धा ती	धा धा	तिर किट
DhaaTee	DhaaTee	DhaaDhaa	TiRaKiTa

धा ती DhaaTee	धा ती DhaaTee	धा धा DhaaDhaa	तु ना TooNaa
ता ती TaaTee	ता ती TaaTee	ता ता TaaTaa	ति र कि ट TiRaKiTa
धा ती DhaaTee	धा ती DhaaTee	धा धा DhaaDhaa	धिं ना DhinNaa

Variation #1

धा ती DhaaTee	धा ती DhaaTee	धा धा DhaaDhaa	ति र कि ट TiRaKiTa
धा ती DhaaTee	धा ती DhaaTee	धा धा DhaaDhaa	ति र कि ट TiRaKiTa
धा ती DhaaTee	धा ती DhaaTee	धा धा DhaaDhaa	ति र कि ट TiRaKiTa
धा ती DhaaTee	धा ती DhaaTee	धा धा DhaaDhaa	तु ना TooNaa
ता ती TaaTee	ता ती TaaTee	ता ता TaaTaa	ति र कि ट TiRaKiTa
ता ती TaaTee	ता ती TaaTee	ता ता TaaTaa	ति र कि ट TiRaKiTa
धा ती DhaaTee	धा ती DhaaTee	धा धा DhaaDhaa	ति र कि ट TiRaKiTa

♩♩ धा ती
DhaaTee

♩♩ धा ती
DhaaTee

♩♩ धा धा
DhaaDhaa

♩♩ धिं ना
DhinNaa

Variation #2

♩♩ धा ती
DhaaTee

♩♩ धा ती
DhaaTee

♩♩ धा धा
DhaaDhaa

♫♫ ति र कि ट
TiRaKiTa

♩♩ धा ती
DhaaTee

♩♩ धा ती
DhaaTee

♩♩ धा धा
DhaaDhaa

♩♩ तू ना
TooNaa

♩♩ धा ती
DhaaTee

♩♩ धा ती
DhaaTee

♩♩ धा धा
DhaaDhaa

♩♩ धिं ना
DhinNaa

♩♩ धा ती
DhaaTee

♩♩ धा ती
DhaaTee

♩♩ धा धा
DhaaDhaa

♩♩ तू ना
TooNaa

♩♩ ता ती
TaaTee

♩♩ ता ती
TaaTee

♩♩ ता ता
TaaTaa

♫♫ ति र कि ट
TiRaKiTa

♩♩ धा ती
DhaaTee

♩♩ धा ती
DhaaTee

♩♩ धा धा
DhaaDhaa

♩♩ धिं ना
DhinNaa

♩♩ धा ती
DhaaTee

♩♩ धा ती
DhaaTee

♩♩ धा धा
DhaaDhaa

♩♩ तू ना
TooNaa

♩♩ धा ती
DhaaTee

♩♩ धा ती
DhaaTee

♩♩ धा धा
DhaaDhaa

♩♩ धिं ना
DhinNaa

Tihai

धा ती,	धा ती,	धा धा,	ति र कि ट,	धा - , - - ,
DhaaTee	DhaaTee	DhaaDhaa	TiRaKiTa	Dhaa

धा ती,	धा ती,	धा धा,	ति र कि ट,	धा - , - - ,
DhaaTee	DhaaTee	DhaaDhaa	TiRaKiTa	Dhaa

धा ती,	धा ती,	धा धा,	ति र कि ट,	ˣधा धिं धिं धा |
DhaaTee	DhaaTee	DhaaDhaa	TiRa KiTa	Dhaa Dhin Dhin Dhaa

We mentioned earlier that the term "kaida" means a system of rules. However we never really discussed what these rules were. It would have been confusing to bring them up earlier because a new student simply doesn't have the experience to make sense of them. However, now that we have gone over a few kaidas it is a good time to discuss them. At this point the rules are probably understood intuitively, but we may still restate them:

1. The overall structure is: theka, introduction (i.e. half tempo), theme (full tempo, usually twice), variations, tihai, return to theka. I believe that this is self explanatory given the previous examples.

2. No bols should be introduced that are not in our theme. Again I believe that given the previous examples this is very clear. However there is a certain amount of latitude. Notice that in the third variation of both our first and second kaida there is the bol *Tee*. At first this may appear to be a new bol but it really isn't. If one looks closely, it is merely the extraction of the first stroke of *TiTa*. Had we introduced *TiRaKiTa* into any of the variations of the first kaida, then that would have constituted a violation of this cardinal rule of kaida.

3. The variations should proceed in a logical, mathematical process. The kaida may be thought of as a poem in rhythm. Let us first look at the limerick. In this poetic form there is a structure which may be described as A, A, B, B, A.

A	There was an old soldier of Bister
A	Went walking one day with his sister
B	When a cow at one poke
B	Tossed her into an oak
A	Before the old gentleman missed her

46

If we look at the previous kaidas there was also a definite structure. If we take Kaida #1 as an example, the basic theme has this structure.

A   Dhaa Dhaa Ti Ta
B   Dhaa Dhaa Tun Naa
A   Taa   Taa   Ti Ta
B   Dhaa Dhaa Dhin Naa

If we extend our analysis further we see that the first variation has the structure: AAABAAAB, the second variation has the structure ABBBABBB. The third variation is somewhat different. The third variation shows how we have broken the earlier A, B structure down, recombined them, then gone on to produce further variations. This too is mathematical and logical, but is perhaps beyond the scope of this introductory book.

4. Every pattern should be played twice. In all of the previous examples the first section (e.g., AAAB) will be reflected back in another iteration. The first iteration will be characterized by the use of resonant left-hand strokes; this is called "bhari". The second section will be characterized by the absence of resonant left-hand strokes; this is called "khali".

Now that we have a working knowledge of kaidas, let us look at a more difficult one.

KAIDA #4 (Nattu Khan's Kaida)

This kaida is said to have been composed by Nattu Khan. He was a great tabla player of the Dilli gharana (Delhi school). It is said that he is the originator of the kaida.

Listen to track 56 to hear Kaida #4

Theka

×धा	धिं	धिं	धा		²धा	धिं	धिं	धा	
Dhaa	Dhin	Dhin	Dhaa	Dhaa	Dhin	Dhin	Dhaa

°धा	तिं	तिं	ना		³ना	धिं	धिं	धा	
Dhaa	Tin	Tin	Naa	Naa	Dhin	Dhin	Dhaa

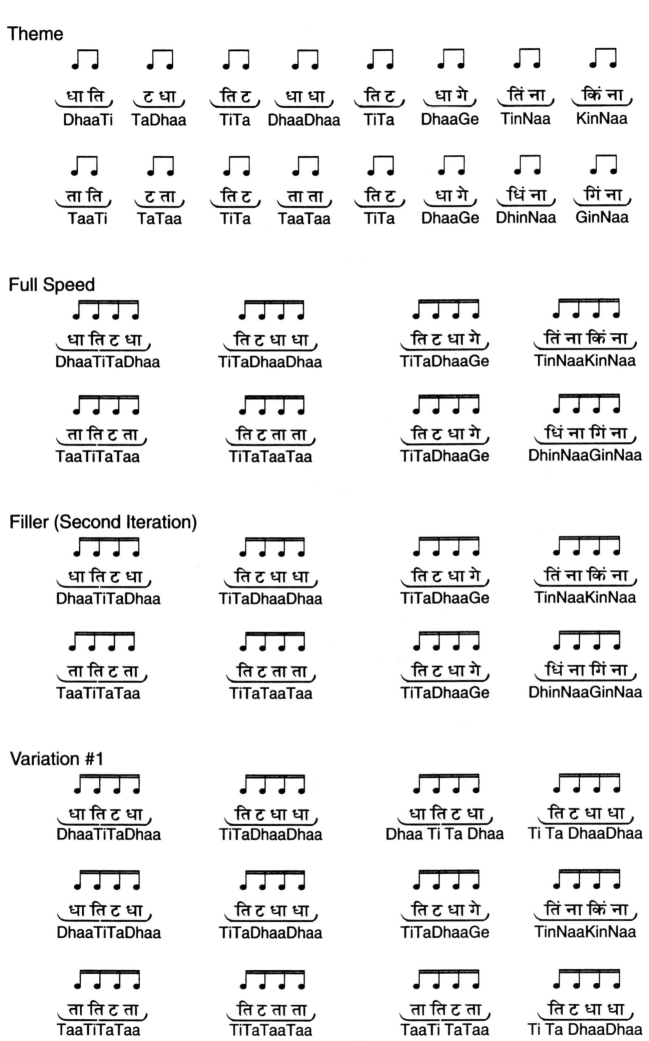

48

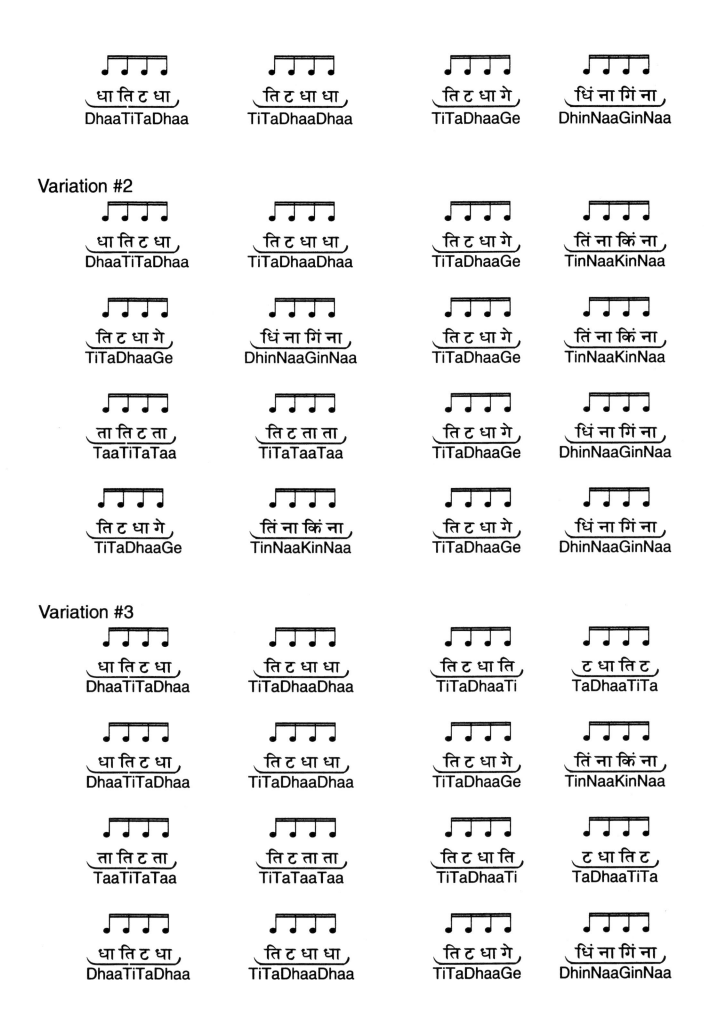

Variation #4

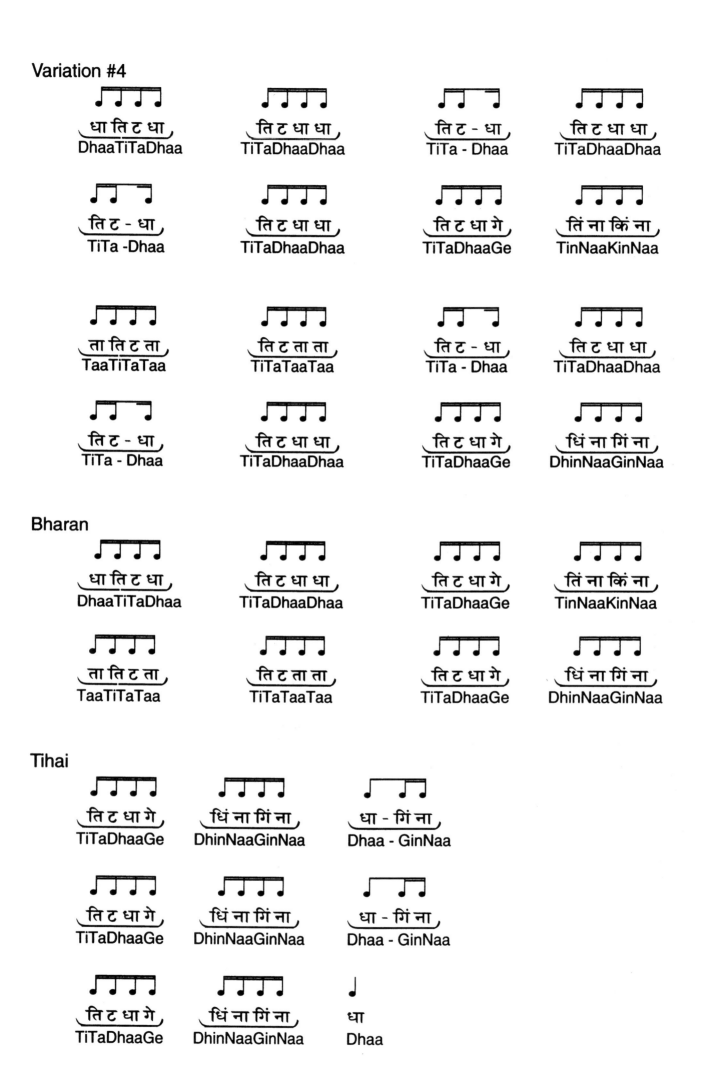

धा ति ट धा
DhaaTiTaDhaa

ति ट धा धा
TiTaDhaaDhaa

ति ट - धा
TiTa - Dhaa

ति ट धा धा
TiTaDhaaDhaa

ति ट - धा
TiTa -Dhaa

ति ट धा धा
TiTaDhaaDhaa

ति ट धा गे
TiTaDhaaGe

तिं ना किं ना
TinNaaKinNaa

ता ति ट ता
TaaTiTaaTaa

ति ट ता ता
TiTaTaaTaa

ति ट - धा
TiTa - Dhaa

ति ट धा धा
TiTaDhaaDhaa

ति ट - धा
TiTa - Dhaa

ति ट धा धा
TiTaDhaaDhaa

ति ट धा गे
TiTaDhaaGe

धिं ना गिं ना
DhinNaaGinNaa

Bharan

धा ति ट धा
DhaaTiTaDhaa

ति ट धा धा
TiTaDhaaDhaa

ति ट धा गे
TiTaDhaaGe

तिं ना किं ना
TinNaaKinNaa

ता ति ट ता
TaaTiTaaTaa

ति ट ता ता
TiTaTaaTaa

ति ट धा गे
TiTaDhaaGe

धिं ना गिं ना
DhinNaaGinNaa

Tihai

ति ट धा गे
TiTaDhaaGe

धिं ना गिं ना
DhinNaaGinNaa

धा - गिं ना
Dhaa - GinNaa

ति ट धा गे
TiTaDhaaGe

धिं ना गिं ना
DhinNaaGinNaa

धा - गिं ना
Dhaa - GinNaa

ति ट धा गे
TiTaDhaaGe

धिं ना गिं ना
DhinNaaGinNaa

धा
Dhaa

MORE TALS, THEKAS, AND PRAKAR

We have already discussed the concept of tal, and theka in an earlier section. We saw that the tal is the rhythmic concept, while theka is the basic "groove". In this section we will return to the same topic and learn a few new ones.

We will also learned a new concept called "prakar". "Prakar" is really just variations upon the theka. Whenever we make any changes to the theka at all, whether to make it sound more interesting or easier to play, the changed version is called a prakar.

PUNJABI THEKA (SITAR KHANI)

16 matras (4+4+4+4) - Punjabi theka is also called "sitarkhani" or sometimes "adha"; but the latter is incorrect. Punjabi theka is very similar to tintal in that it is composed of four vibhags of four matras each. Like tintal, this too is defined as: clap, clap, wave, and clap. The rhythm is very peculiar, so listen very carefully to the recorded version to get the beat correct. It is often easier to get a handle on it by saying 123,123,12.

Counting exercise
12 31 23 12 | 12 31 23 12 | 12 31 23 12 | 12 31 23 12

Theka

| ♩. | ♩. | ♩ | ♩. | ♩. | ♩ | ♩. | ♩. | ♩ | ♩. | ♩. | ♩ |

×धा - धिं - धा | ²धा - धिं - धा | ०धा - तिं - ना | ³ना - धिं - धा |
Dhaa Dhin Dhaa   Dhaa Dhin Dhaa   Dhaa Tin Naa   Naa Dhin Dhaa

The above version is the simple version, however we often wish to embellish it. Here is a prakar (embellished version) of punjabi theka

Prakar of Punjabi theka

♩ ♫ 7♪ ♩   ♩ ♫ 7♪ ♩

×धा ग धी - ग धा | ²धा ग धी - ग धा |
Dhaa GaDhee Ga Dhaa   Dhaa GaDhee Ga Dhaa

♩ ♫ 7♪ ♩   ♩ ♫ 7♪ ♩

०धा क ती - क ना | ³ना ग धी - ग धा |
Dhaa KaTee Ka Naa   Naa GaDhee Ga Dhaa

> Listen to track 57 to hear Punjabi theka
>
> Listen to track 58 to hear prakar of Punjabi theka

EKTAL

12 matras (2+2+2+2+2+2) -This tal has six vibhags of two matras each with the arrangement of: clap, wave, clap, wave, clap, clap. Although this is the traditionally accepted clapping arrangement, the internal structure of the theka follows a six / six structure. The technique is straight-forward except for one section. The expression *ToonNaaKatTaa* has an interpretation which shows the influence of pakhawaj. This is a characteristic of Purbi compositions. It was noted earlier that *Toon* is played just like *Too; Naa* is standard. *Kat* is unusual; in this context the *Kat* is played with the right hand. *Taa* is also different from what we have played before. This *Taa* is played off the maidan instead of the chat (see page 12 for diagram of tabla). It is often easier to think of this style of *Taa* as being similar to *Tin* except much more forceful. The different technique has had some interesting consequences. Just as using words such as "ain't" marks a person as being uneducated, in the same way an incorrect usage of *ToonNaaKatTaa* is a broadly recognized sign of poor training. Take warning and watch this very carefully!

Counting Exercises #1

^{x}1   2 | ^{o}1   2 | ^{2}1   2 |

^{o}1   2 | ^{3}1   2 | ^{4}1   2 |

Counting Exercises #2

^{x}1   2 | ^{o}3   4 | ^{2}5   6 |

^{o}7   8 | ^{3}9   10 | ^{4}11   12 |

Ektal Theka

ˣधिं	धिं	° धा गे	तिर किट	²तूं	ना
Dhin	Dhin	DhaaGe	TiRaKiTa	Toon	Naa

°कत्	ता	³ धा गे	तिर किट	⁴धिं	ना
Kat	Taa	DhaaGe	TiRaKiTa	Dhin	Naa

Slow Ektal - Although Ektal is theoretically 12 matras, this version is so slow that it is more convenient to think of it as being 48 matras. Here is a common prakar.

धिं	1	2	गे गे	धिं	1	2	धिं	
Dhin	1	2	GeGe	Dhin	1	2	Dhin
धा	-	धा	गे गे	ति	रि	कि	ट	
Dhaa	-	Dhaa	GeGe	Ti	Ri	Ki	Ta
तूं	1	2	तिं	ना	-	ना	ना ना	
Toon	1	2	Tin	Naa	-	Naa	NaaNaa
कत्	1	2	के के	तिं	1	2	धिं	
Kat	1	2	KeKe	Tin (Ta)	1	2	Dhin
धा	-	धा	गे गे	ति	रि	कि	ट	
Dhaa	-	Dhaa	GeGe	Ti	Ri	Ki	Ta
धिं	1	2	धिं	धा	-	धा	धा धा	
Dhin	1	2	Dhin	Dhaa	-	Dhaa	DhaaDhaa

Listen to track 60
to hear Slow Ektal

Fast Ektal - Here is a prakar of ektal which is easy to play at high speed.

Listen to track 61
to hear Fast Ektal

KAHERAVA TAL

8 matras (4+4) - This is one of the most common tals in northern India. Semi-classical, light, filmi, or folk styles use it extensively.

Counting Exercises #1

^{x}1   2   3   4 | ^{o}1   2   3   4 |

Counting Exercises #2

^{x}1   2   3   4 | ^{o}5   6   7   8 |

Listen to track 62
to hear Kaherava

Kaherava theka:

ˣधा गे ना ती | °ना क धिं ना |
Dhaa Ge   Naa Tee   Naa Ka   Dhin Naa

Kaherava Tal (Prakar #1)

ˣधा धिं धा धिं | °धा तूं नाक तिट |
Dhaa Dhin Dhaa Dhin   Dhaa Toon NaaKaTiTa

Kaherava Tal (Prakar #2)

ˣधा धिं धा धिं |
Dhaa Dhin Dhaa Dhin

°धा तूं नाक तिरकिट |
Dhaa Toon NaaKa TiRaKiTa

The following may
be heard on the
recording

track 63 - Kaherava #1
track 64 - Kaherava #2

TINTAL PRAKARS

We introduced tintal earlier in this book (pg. 26). It has a structure of four measures of four beats each. It is designated with a clap, clap, wave, clap. The basic theka goes like this:

Tintal Theka

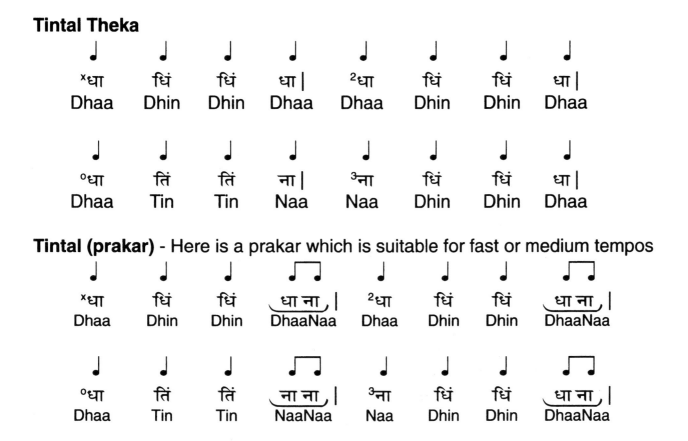

धा	धिं	धिं	धा	धा	धिं	धिं	धा
Dhaa	Dhin	Dhin	Dhaa	Dhaa	Dhin	Dhin	Dhaa

धा	तिं	तिं	ना	ना	धिं	धिं	धा
Dhaa	Tin	Tin	Naa	Naa	Dhin	Dhin	Dhaa

Tintal (prakar) - Here is a prakar which is suitable for fast or medium tempos

धा	धिं	धिं	धा ना	धा	धिं	धिं	धा ना
Dhaa	Dhin	Dhin	DhaaNaa	Dhaa	Dhin	Dhin	DhaaNaa

धा	तिं	तिं	ना ना	ना	धिं	धिं	धा ना
Dhaa	Tin	Tin	NaaNaa	Naa	Dhin	Dhin	DhaaNaa

Tintal (slow prakar) - Here is a very slow tintal prakar.

धा	तिरकिट	धिं धिं	धा ती
Dhaa	TiRaKiTa	DhinDhin	DhaaTee

धा ना	धिं - - कृ	धिं धिं	धा ती
DhaaNaa	DhinKra	DhinDhin	DhaaTee

धा ना	तिं - - कृ	तिं तिं	ना - तिट
DhaaNaa	Tin Kra	TinTin	Naa TiTa

ना क तिट	धिं - तिट	धिं धिं	धा गे तिट
NaaKaTiTa	Dhin TiTa	DhinDhin	DhaaGeTiTa

The following may be heard on the recording

track 65 -
Tintal prakar

track 66 -
Slow Tintal

DADRA PRAKARS

Dadra tal was also introduced earlier (pg. 27). It is composed of two vibhags of three matras each. It is designated by a clap, wave. As previously mentioned its theka is:

Theka

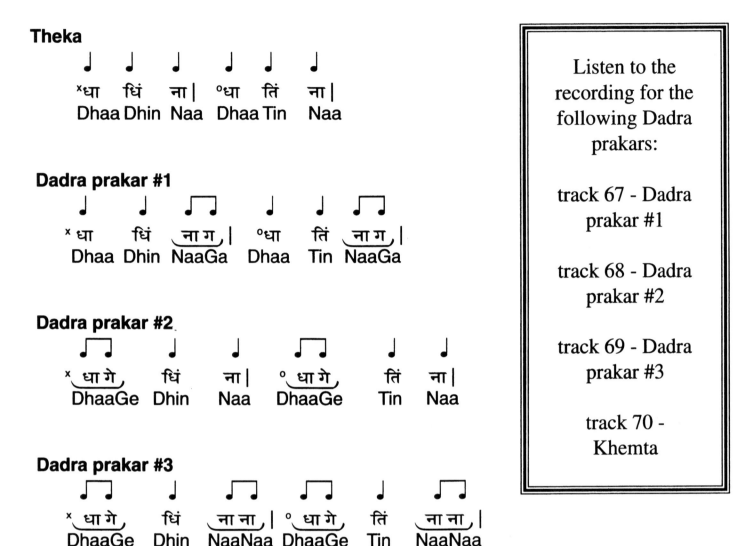

Dadra prakar #1

Dadra prakar #2

Dadra prakar #3

> Listen to the recording for the following Dadra prakars:
>
> track 67 - Dadra prakar #1
>
> track 68 - Dadra prakar #2
>
> track 69 - Dadra prakar #3
>
> track 70 - Khemta

Khemta - There is a style of dadra tal which is so common and so formalized that it is sometimes considered to be a separate tal. It is usually called "khemta". Its basic structure is like this.

JHAPTAL PRAKARS

Jhaptal was discussed in an earlier section (pg. 27). As mentioned earlier it is a ten beat tal that is divided into four vibhags of two beats, three beats, two beats, three beats respectively. Its basic theka is:

Theka

Dhin Naa Dhin Dhin Naa Tin Naa Dhin Dhin Naa

Jhaptal (prakar #1)

Dhin NaaNaa Dhin Dhin NaaNaa

Toon NaaNaa DhinDhin NaaNaa

Jhaptal (prakar #2)

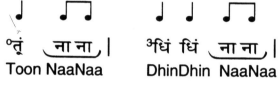

Dhin NaaNaa Dhin DhinDhin NaaNaa

Toon NaaNaa Dhin DhinDhin NaaNaa

Jhaptal (prakar #3)

Dhin Naa NaaNaa Dhin -- Kra DhinDhin NaaNaa

Tin Naa NaaNaa Dhin -- Kra DhinDhin NaaNaa

Listen to the recording for the following prakars:

track 71 - Jhaptal prakar #1

track 72 - Jhaptal prakar #2

track 73 - Jhaptal prakar #3

RUPAK TAL PRAKARS

Rupak tal was mentioned earlier (pg. 28). It was noted that rupak is a seven-matra tal composed of three vibhags of three-beats, two-beats and two-beats respectively. It is denoted by wave, clap, clap. Its theka is:

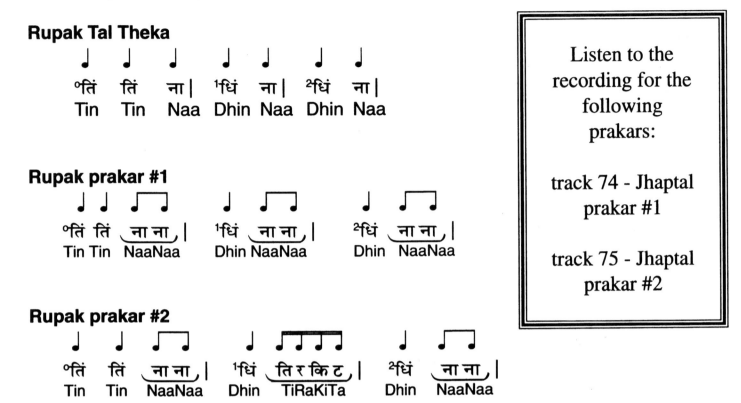

Rupak Tal Theka

°तिं तिं ना | ¹धिं ना | ²धिं ना |
Tin   Tin   Naa Dhin Naa Dhin Naa

Rupak prakar #1

°तिं तिं ना ना, | ¹धिं ना ना, | ²धिं ना ना, |
Tin   Tin NaaNaa   Dhin NaaNaa   Dhin   NaaNaa

Rupak prakar #2

°तिं तिं ना ना, | ¹धिं तिर किट, | ²धिं ना ना, |
Tin   Tin   NaaNaa   Dhin TiRaKiTa   Dhin   NaaNaa

> Listen to the recording for the following prakars:
>
> track 74 - Jhaptal prakar #1
>
> track 75 - Jhaptal prakar #2

PURBI BAJ

At the beginning of this book we mentioned that there were two overall techniques to tabla. There is the pure tabla technique which is called the Delhi technique or "Dilli baj" then there is another style which is called "Purbi baj" (literally the "Eastern style of playing"). In the old days it seems that every gharana had its own baj. However improvements in communication and transportation have mixed the various techniques to the point that today there are really only two overall techniques. Perhaps in another hundred years there may be no separate bajs at all.

We have also mentioned that it is imperative for a modern performer to be comfortable with both techniques, here are the reasons. Dilli baj is characterized by extreme flexibility. Most combinations of bols can be executed without much trouble. It is also known for its delicacy. But there is a downside to this delicacy; after a while of uninterrupted Dilli technique, the performance sounds weak and ineffective. The Purbi technique on the other hand is extremely powerful and majestic, it gets the audiences attention and holds it. However the Purbi baj is not without its shortcomings. A long performance of pure Purbi technique after a while becomes tiresome, and lacking in grace. Furthermore there are limited combinations of bols which can be executed.

Therefore the modern generation of tabla players have a facility in both styles. The Dilli style gives speed, and delicacy, while the Purbi style gives power and majesty. Unfortunately there is no standard among the teachers as how it is to be taught. Some teach the Purbi style first and then introduce the Dilli techniques; some will teach the Dilli technique first. We have taken the latter approach, we started with Dilli baj, now it is time to introduce the Purbi baj.

In a nutshell we can say that the Purbi baj shows a strong influence of the pakhawaj. Pakhawaj is a two headed drum used in the royal courts in the last few centuries. In the old days the royal courts did not have electronic sound systems (duh!). Therefore the pakhawaj had to be very loud. Therefore we can attain more power by applying this technique to the tabla.

Pakhawaj (Mridang)

59

However there are fundamental differences between the tabla and the pakhawaj. The heads of the pakhawaj are very large, while the tabla dayan is much smaller. Furthermore the heads of the pakhawaj are pointing horizontally while the heads of the tabla point vertically. The result is that it is not practical to apply the pakhawaj technique to the tabla without change. Therefore numerous small changes were introduced to create the technique that today we call Purbi baj. Let us start with a few exercises to acquaint ourselves with this technique.

Purbi Taa - We will start by learning the distinction between *Taa* and *Naa*. Up to now we have said that *Naa* and *Taa* are the same. This is true in the Dilli baj but there is a distinct difference between *Taa* and *Naa* in the Purbi baj. Within this technique *Naa* is exactly the same as it was in the Dilli style (i.e., struck sharply on the chat with the index finger). However *Taa* is different. Purbi *Taa* is played loudly in the maidan (refer to pg. 12 to refresh yourself on the parts of the pudi). Here is an exercise:

Exercise 47.

ता - ना ना
Taa   Naa Naa

Purbi Dhaa - Earlier we implied that since *Naa* and *Taa* were the same, *Dhaa* could be seen as a combination of *Naa* and *Ga*. This is not actually true. Dhaa is really a combination of *Taa* and *Ga*. Since our *Taa* is different in the Purbi system then it follows that *Dhaa* should also be different. Here is an exercise to become comfortable with Purbi *Dhaa*:

> Listen to the recording for the following exercises:
>
> track 76 - Exercise #47
>
> track 77 - Exercise #48

Exercise 48.

धा धा धा धा
Dhaa Dhaa Dhaa Dhaa

Purbi Ga and its Associated Strokes - It was the tendency in our old interpretations of the Purbi baj that the bayan in *Ga, Dhaa, Dhin* etc. was not highly modulated. If you wish to adhere strictly to the Purbi style you may wish to keep the left hand in such strokes unmodulated. However contemporary practice is go right ahead and modulate these strokes as much as you wish.

Purbi TiTa - Purbi *TiTa* is very different from the Dilli version. The Purbi style starts with all the last three fingers (i.e., middle, ring, and little finger), then comes in with the index finger.

Exercise 49.   ♩   ♩   ♩   ♩

तिं   ट   तिं   ट
Ti   Ta   Ti   Ta

Exercise 50.   ♩   ♩   ♩

धा   -   तिं   ट
Dhaa   Ti   Ta

Exercise 51.   ♩   ♩   ♩

धा   तिं   ट   -
Dhaa Ti   Ta

Listen to the recording for the following exercises:

track 78 - Exercise #49
track 79 - Exercise #50
track 80 - Exercise #51

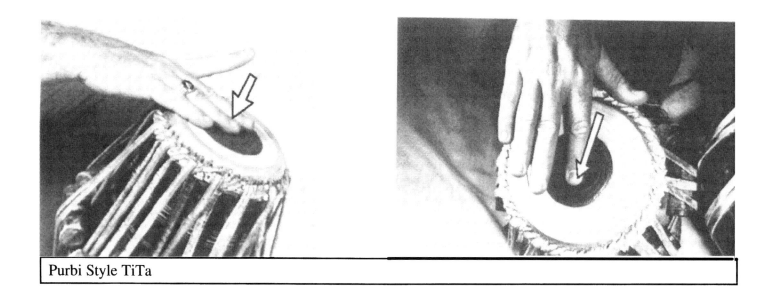

Purbi Style TiTa

Purbi TiRaKiTa - Purbi *TiRaKiTa* is also different. This style of *TiRaKiTa* starts out with the last three fingers, then comes down with the index finger (right hand), then a standard *Ka* of the left hand, and finally ends with the last three fingers of the right hand.

Let us return to some of our older exercises, but this time we will use a Purbi technique.

Here are some exercises.

Exercise 52.   ♩   ♩   ♩   ♩

तिं   र   कि   ट
Ti   Ra   Ki   Ta

Listen to track 81
for Exercise #52

This last exercise clearly underscores the major weakness of the Purbi baj. It is a difficult matter to wrap back around to play successive *TiRaKiTa*s. However keep on and later you will see the strengths of this style.

Exercise 53.

धा   धा   तिर   किट
Dhaa Dhaa   Ti Ra   Ki Ta

Listen to track 82
for Exercise #53

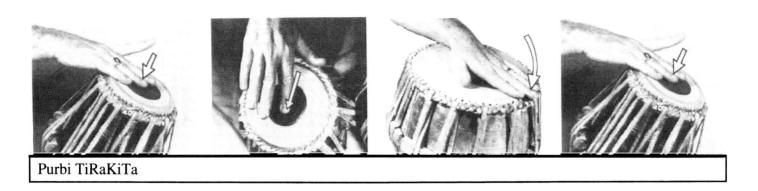

Purbi TiRaKiTa

TiRaKiTaTaKa (तिर किट त क) - This is a new bol. Bols like this clearly show the strength of the Purbi baj. The technique is to play the first *Ti Ra Kit Ta* exactly as in the previous example; however we then append a *TaKa* to it by playing the index finger of the right hand, and them coming down with the left hand *Ka*. Therefore its technique is illustrated below.

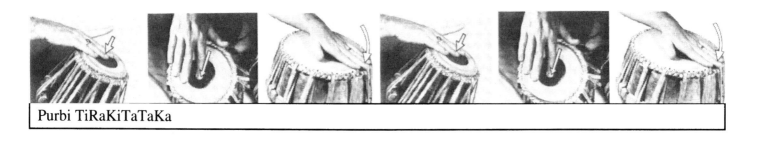

Purbi TiRaKiTaTaKa

Here are a couple of exercises:

Exercise 54.

धा   तिर   किट   तक
Dhaa   Ti Ra   Ki Ta   TaKa

Listen to track 83
for Exercise #54

Exercise 55.

धा धा तिर किट तक तिर किट तक
Dhaa Dhaa Ti Ra Ki Ta TaKa Ti Ra Ki Ta TaKa

This last exercise shows very nicely the strength of this technique. Although *TiRaKiTa* does not extend well, Bols such as *TiRaKiTaTaKa* extend very well so we may build up bols such as:

TiRaKiTaTaKaTiRaKiTa,
TiRaKiTaTaKaTiRaKiTaTaKa,
TiRaKiTaTaKaTiRaKiTaTaKaTiRaKiTa
TiRaKiTaTaKaTiRaKiTaTaKaTiRaKiTaTaKa
TiRaKiTaTaKaTiRaKiTaTaKaTiRaKiTaTaKaTiRaKiTa
TiRaKiTaTaKaTiRaKiTaTaKaTiRaKiTaTaKaTiRaKiTaTaKa (etc.)

```
Listen to track 84
for Exercise #55
```

STILL MORE BOLS

Let us learn a few more bols. These will be both single bols as well as bol expressions (compound bols).

Ki Ra Naa Ka (कि ड् ना क) **or Ki Da Naa Ka** (कि ड ना क) - This is a common expression which has an interesting interplay between the various fingers of the left and right hands. *Ki* is nothing more than a standard *Ka*; *Ra* is played with last two fingers of the right hand; *Naa* is a standard; and *Ka* is standard.

Exercise 56.

कि	ड्	ना	क
Ki	Ra	Naa	Ka

Listen to track 85
for Exercise #56

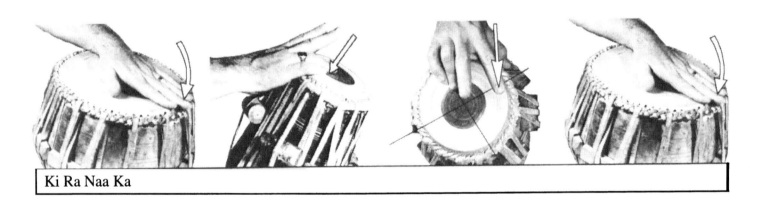

Ki Ra Naa Ka

Taa - Ti Ta Ki Ra Naa Ka (ता - ति ट कि ड ना क) - This is also a common expression. One can see that it is merely *KiRaNaaKa* with a *Taa -TiTa* attached to it. The *Taa* is a standard Dilli *Taa* (i.e., *Naa*), while the *TiTa* may be either Dilli or Purbi (if you do not have a personal preference, you will find the Dilli style is fastest). The *KiRaNaaKa* is exactly like the one we played in the previous exercise.

Exercise 57.

ता	-	ति	ट	कि	ड्	ना	क
Taa	-	Ti	Ta	Ki	Ra	Naa	Ka

Listen to track 86
for Exercise #57

Gi Ra Naa Ga (गि ड़ ना ग) **or Gi Da Naa Ga** (गि ड ना ग) - This is similar to *KiRaNaaKa* except that the closed sounding *Ka*s have been replaced by open, resonant *Ga*s. There is a little twist to the technique because the first *Gi* is played by using a two-finger *Ga* while the last *Ga* is played by using a one-finger version. If one plays this exercise for a few minutes, the technical reason for this is readily apparent. Alternating between the two different types of *Ga*s allows for greater speed with decreased fatigue.

Exercise 58.

♩	♩	♩	♩
गि	ड़	ना	ग
Gi	Ra	Naa	Ga
2			1

Listen to track 87
for Exercise #58

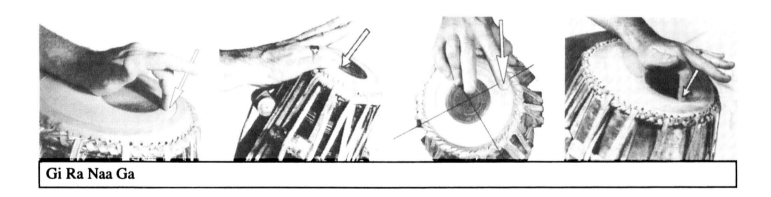

Gi Ra Naa Ga

Dhaa - Ti Ta Gi Ra Naa Ga (धा - ति ट गि ड़ ना ग) - This is nothing but the last exercise with *Dhaa - TiTa* added to it.

Exercise 59.

♩		♩	♩	♩	♩	♩	♩
धा	-	ति	ट	गि	ड़	ना	ग
Dhaa		Ti	Ta	Gi	Ra	Naa	Ga

Listen to track 88
for Exercise #59

A mukhada is a simple embellishment ending on the sam (the first beat of the cycle). They may be played in any style, either Dilli or Purbi. There is a tendency to give preference to the Purbi baj for the mukhadas. This is only a tendency and is not a rule. Here are some simple mukhadas in tintal of 16 beats:

Mukhada #1

ˣधा धिं धिं धा | ²धा धिं धिं धा |
Dhaa Dhin Dhin Dhaa Dhaa Dhin Dhin Dhaa

°धा तिं तिं ना | ³धा धा तिर किट |
Dhaa Tin Tin Naa Dhaa Dhaa TiRa KiTa

> Listen to the recording for the following mukhadas:
>
> track 89 - Mukhada #1
>
> track 90 - Mukhada #2
>
> track 91 - Mukhada #3

Mukhada #2

ˣधा धिं धिं धा | ²धा धिं धिं धा |
Dhaa Dhin Dhin Dhaa Dhaa Dhin Dhin Dhaa

°धा तिं तिं ना | ³ता ता तिरकिट धा धा तिरकिट |
Dhaa Tin Tin Naa TaaTaa TiRaKiTa DhaaDhaa TiRaKiTa

Mukhada #3

ˣधा धिं धिं धा | ²धा धिं धिं धा |
Dhaa Dhin Dhin Dhaa Dhaa Dhin Dhin Dhaa

°धा तिं तिं ना | ³तिट धा - तिर किट धा - तिरकिट |
Dhaa Tin Tin Naa TiTa Dhaa TiRa KiTaDhaa TiRaKiTa

Mukhada #4

Mukhada #5

Mukhada #6

Mukhada #7

Listen to the recording for the following mukhadas:

track 92 - Mukhada #4

track 93 - Mukhada #5

track 94 - Mukhada #6

track 95 - Mukhada #7

67

CONCLUSION

In this modest little book we have tried to give a basic introduction to the tabla. There is much that we have not been able to cover. Terms such as rela, laggi, gat, chakradar may not mean anything to the student at this point. However they all point to a vast area of technique and compositional theory that we could not even touch upon.

But that is ok. This book is not designed to be an all-inclusive discussion of the subject. It is just the first steps in a long journey. So now what is next?

The next thing is practice; practice, practice. It is important that you don't just do one type of practice. Try practicing with a metronome. Try practicing without a metronome. Practice with recorded music. Do anything to broaden your perspective on the subject.

The most important practice of all is with other live musicians. I do not presume to tell you what artistic direction you should take. Some of you have interest in lighter forms of music such as filmi, gazal, or folk music. Some of you may have interest in classical. There are even those of you who have interested in jazz or fusion. These are all legitimate genre.

Do not forget that the mechanics of performing with live musicians is going to be different from one genre to another. It will even be different from one musician to another. There is no substitute for a broad background of practice and experience.

So keep busy and we hope that you will progress in this beautiful Indian instrument.

OTHER SOURCES OF INFORMATION

INTERNET SOURCES

The Tabla Site - http://chandrakantha.com/tablasite - articles, discussion forum and more.

Tabla.com - http://www.tabla.com - Information, books, CDs, tablas

Introduction to North Indian Music - http://chandrakantha.com/articles/indian_music/ -hypertext introduction to North Indian music.

David and Chandrakantha Courtney's Homepage - http://chandrakantha.com/forums/ , The author's personal Homepage.

Indian Music Forums - http://chandrakantha.com/forums/ - Forums for the tabla and other aspects of Indian music.

SUPPLIERS OF TABLA

USA and Canada
This is just a partial list, for an updated list check out
http://chandrakantha.com/tablasite/supply.html

Ali Akbar College of Music, 215 West End Ave., San Rafael, CA 94901-2645, USA, (415) 454 6264 (tel), (415) 454 9396 (fax), (800) 74 TABLA, store@aacm.org, http://www.aacm.org/store.html

Apollo's Axes, Apollo's Axes, LLC, 15603 Cassandra Place, Tampa, FL 33624, USA, Tel (800) 827 9196, http://www.apollosaxes.com

Bang a Drum, 1255 S. La Brea Ave. Los Angeles, CA 90019, USA, (800)495-1109, http://www.bangadrum.com, service@bangadrum.com

Buckingham Music, 13432 Albania Way, Austin, TX 78729, USA, 512-249-8995, http://www.buckinghammusic.com, paula@buckinghammusic.com

Dulhan Boutique Inc., 2637 1/2 - 39 W. Devon Ave, Chicago, IL, 60659, USA, (773) 262 5829 (tel), (773) 274 4949 (tel)

Encinitas Imports, 949 2nd St., Encinitas, CA 92024, USA, (866) 334-9589 (tel), info@encinitasimports.com, http://www.encinitasimports.com/

House of Raga, 462 McNicoll Ave., Willowdale, Ont, M2H 2E1, Canada, (877) 817-7242 (tel), (416) 251 4036 (fax), sales@houseofraga.com, http://www.houseofraga.com/

Kala Kendar Ltd., 1440 Gerrard Street East : 2nd Floor (upstairs) : Toronto Ontario Canada : M4L 1Z8, attn. Mickey Khorana, (Tel) 416 463-3111, (Fax)416 463-7784, E-Mail info@kalakendar.com, http://www.kalakendar.com

Krishna Culture, Houston Tx, 77018, USA, (800) 829 2579 (tel), (713) 290 8720 (fax), http://www.krishnaculture.com

Rhythm Fusion, 1541 C Pacific Ave, Santa Cruz, CA 95060, USA, (831) 423 2048 (tel), (831) 423 2073 (fax), rhythm@rhythmfusion.com, http://wwwRhythmfusion.com

Sacred Rites, attn. Kelly McCabe, 8 N. San Francisco St., Flagstaff, AZ 86001, (928) 556 0018 (tel), contact@sacredrites.com, http://www.sacredrites.com/

Shree Ganesh Groceries, 18411 Pioneer Blvd., Artesia, CA 90701, USA, (562) 924 1499 (tel), (562) 924 5107 (fax)

Toko Imports, attn. Tom Kozlowski, DeWitt Mall, 215 N. Cayuga St., Ithaca NY 14850, USA, (607) 277 3780 (tel)

Tzara International, 7709 S. W. Pfaffle St. #23, Portland, OR 97223, USA, (888) 282 1930 (tel), (206) 888 4026 (fax) sales@tabla.com, http://tabla.com/

Voyager's Dream, 1306 W. Hickory, Denton, TX 76201, USA, (940) 381 2769 (tel), info@voyagersdream.com, http://www.voyagersdream.com

Europe

Bina Musicals & Boutique Centre - 31-33 The Green : Middlesex, UB24AN : United Kingdom, 44 181 511 5904 (tel)

Earth Vibe Music - 53 Brentwood Road : Brighton : Sussex : BN1 7ET, 44 (0) 1273 554043, gavin@earthvibemusic.com, http://www.earthvibemusic.com/

Jas Musicals Ltd. - 124 The Broadway, : Southall, : Middlesex, : UB1 1QF (U.K.) London, 4 (0)208 574 2686, info@jas-musicals.com, http://www.jas-musicals.com/

Knock on Wood - 13 Eastgate : Leeds LS2 7LY : United Kingdom, +44(0)113 242 9146 (Tel / Fax), info@knockonwood.co.uk, http://www.knockonwood.co.uk/

Musik Produktiv, Griesfeldstr. 6 2351 Wr. Neudorf, Austria, +43 (0) 2236/62336-0 (Tel) +43 (0) 2236/62336-109 (fax), http://www.musik-produktiv.at, info@musik-produktiv.at

Sarasvati and Narada, Sarasvati : Via Roncaglia 31 : 20146 Milano : Italy, 39 02 4819102 (tel), info@sarasvati.it, http://www.sarasvati.it/

Shemsuddin Import, Kloosterstraat 8c : 5935 CB Steyl : Nederland, 31-(0)77-3736709(tel), 31-(0)77-3732110 (fax) info@shemsuddin.nl, http://www.shemsuddin.nl/

OTHER BOOKS AND ARTICLES

Chaturvedi. B.K.
- no date - How to Play Tabla. New Delhi: Diamond Pocket Books.

Courtney, D.R
1980 Introduction to Tabla, Hyderabad, India: Anand Power Press.

1985 "Tabla Making in the Deccan", Percussive Notes. Vol 23 No 2: pp 33-34. Urbana: Percussive Arts Society.

1988 "The Tabla Puddi", Experimental Musical Instruments. Vol 4 No 4: pp 12-16. Nicasio: EMI.

1991 "Tuning the Tabla: A Psychoacoustic Perspective", Percussive Notes. Vol 29 No 3: pp 59-61. Urbana: Percussive Arts Society.

1992 "New Approaches to Tabla Instruction", Percussive Notes. Vol 30 No 4: pp 27-29. Lawton OK: Percussive Arts Society.

1993 "Mrdangam et Tabla: un Contraste", Percussions: Cahier Bimensiel d'Études et d'Informations sur les Arts de la Percussion. Chailly-en-Biere, France: Vol 28, March/April 1993; pp 11-14.

1993 "An Introduction to Tabla", Modern Drummer. Mt. Morris, IL: October 1993; Vol 17, #10: pp.38-84.

1993 "Repair and Maintenance of Tabla", Percussive Notes, Lawton OK: October 1993; Vol.31, No 7: pp 29-36.

1994 "The Cadenza in North Indian Tabla", Percussive Notes, Lawton OK: August 1994; Vol.32, No 4: pp 54-64.

1995 Fundamentals of Tabla, Houston TX: Sur Sangeet Services.

1999 "Psychoacoustics of the Musical Pitch of Tabla", Journal of Sangeet Research Academy, Calcutta, India Vol 13, No 1, October

2000 Advanced Theory of Tabla, Houston TX: Sur Sangeet Services.

2001 Manufacture and Repair of Tabla, Houston TX: Sur Sangeet Services.

Das, Ram Shankar (Pagaldas)
1967 *Tabla Kaumudi,* (vol. 2). Gwalior, India: Ramchandra Sangeetalaya.

Feldman, Jeffrey M. & Alla Rakha
(no date) *Learning Tabla with Alla Rakha,* Los Angeles: Ravi Shankar Music Circle.
1995 The Tabla Legacy of Taranath Rao. Venice, California. Gigitala.

Ganguly, S.
1981 *Introduction to Tabla,* Delhi, India: B. R. Printers.

Gottlieb, R. S.
1977a *The Major Traditions of North Indian Tabla Drumming,* Munchen, Germany: Musikverlag Emil Katzbichler.
1977b *The Major Traditions of North Indian Tabla Drumming,* Transcriptions :Munchen, Germany: Musikverlag Emil Katzbichler.

Jha, Narayan
1983 *Tal Prabhand: Panch Talon Men Yaman-Kalyan,* Sangeet (Tal Ank). Hathras, India: Sangeet Karyalaya.Vol. 14: Edited by Prabhulal Garg.

Kippen, James
1988 *The Tabla of Lucknow,* Cambridge, Great Britain: Cambridge University Press.

Leake, Jerry
1993 *Indian Influence (Tabla Perspective),* Series A.I.M. Percussion Text (Second Edition). Boston: Rhombus Publishing.

Lele, V.
1983 *Sathsangat,* Puna, India: V. Joshi and Co.

Mrdangacharya, B. D.
1976 *Mrdang-Tabla -Prabhakar,* (vol. 1). Hathras, India: Sangeet Karyalaya.

Mrdangacharya, Bhagavan Das and Ram Shankar Das (Pagaldas)
1977 *Mrdang-Tabla -Prabhakar,* (vol. 2). Hathras, India: Sangeet Karyalaya.

Patnakar, R. G.
1977 *Tal Sopan,* (vol. 2) Bulandshahar, India: Sangeet Kala Kendra.
1978 *Tal Sopan,* (vol. 1) Bulandshahar, India: Sangeet Kala Kendra.

Sharma, Bhagavat Sharan
1973 *Tal Prakash,* Hathras, India: Sangeet Karyalaya.
1977 *Tal Shastra,* Alighar, India: B. A. Electric Press.

Shepherd, F. A.
1976 *Tabla and the Benares Gharana*, Ann Arbor: University Microfilms International. (Ph.D. Dissertation).

Shrivastava, Girish Chandra
1978 *Tal Parichay*, (vol. 2). Alahabad, India: Sangeet Press.
1979 *Tal Parichay*, (vol. 1). Alahabad, India: Sangeet Press.

Singh, Anandram "Tomar"
1978 *Tabla ke Kuchh Aprachalit Bol*, Tal Ank. Hathras, India: Sangeet Karyalaya.

Stewart, R. M.
1974 *The Tabla in Perspective*, Ann Arbor: University Microfilms International. (Ph.D. Dissertation).

Vashisth, Satya Narayan
1977 *Tal Martand*, Hathras, India: Sangeet Karyalaya.
1981 *Kaida aur Peshkar*, Hathras, India: Sangeet Karyalaya.
1982 *Aprachalit Kaiyade aur gaten*, Hathras, India: Sangeet Karyalaya.

GLOSSARY

abhog आभोग - A quaternary theme found in dhrupad and other older vocal forms.

addha tal अद्धा ताल - A tal of 16 beats.

Ajrada अजराड़ा - A village near Meerat.

ajrada baj अजराड़ा बाज - A style of playing originating from Ajrada.

alap आलाप - A slow rhythmless elaboration upon the rag used by vocalists and instrumentalists.

Amir Khusru अमीर खुसरो - Musician during time of Ala-u-Din Khilji.

ang अंग - (lit. limb, or section) A measure, or vibhag.

antara अंतरा - A secondary theme in vocal styles.

ati drut अति द्रुत - Ultra-fast tempo.

ati vilambit अति विलंबित - Ultra slow tempo.

avanaddh अवनद्ध - A membranous percussive instrument (e.g., tabla, dholak, mridang, etc.)

avartan आवर्तन - A cycle of the tal.

avrutti आवृत्ति - See avartan.

azan अज़ां - The Islamic call to prayer.

baaj बाज - See baj.

baaz बाज़ - See baj.

badhi बद्धी - The tasma.

baj बाज - A style of playing (i.e., dilli baj, ajrada baj, etc.).

bal बल - A palta or permutation of rela or kaida.

banarasi baj बनारसी बाज - A style of playing originating in Benares, often considered synonymous to Purbi baj.

band बन्द - (Lit. "closed".) Non-resonant strokes such as Te, Ka, Kat, Tak, etc.

bandish बंदिश - A composition or fixed musical piece.

bant बाँट - Another name for kaida.

banti बाँटी - Another name for kaida.

bayan बायाँ - The large metal left hand drum.

bedum tihai बेदम तिहाई - A tihai in which the three sections are not separated by a pause.

Benares बनारस - A city in North India. A gharana from that city.

bharan भरन - A filler. Something of little theoretical importance used to fill up a certain number of beats.

bhari भरी - (Lit. "full") 1) Clapped, see tali. 2) A section which is characterized by open strokes.

bhatkhande paddhati भातखन्डे पद्धति - The theoretical and notational system of Bhatkhande.

biradari बिरादरी - (Lit. "brotherhood") The relationship that exists between musicians of the same gharana.

bol बोल - The mnemonic syllabi of tabla.

cakkardar - See chakradar.

calan - See chalan.

Carnatic sangeet कर्नाटिक संगीत - The south Indian system of music.

chakradar चकदार - A tihai in which each phrase is a tihai in itself.

chanchar चाँचर - See dipchandi.

chant चाँट - See chat.

chanti चाँटी - See chat.

chart चार्ट - See chat

chat चाट - The outer section of the tabla skin.

chela चेला - A disciple, or student.

chutta छुट्टा - The cushioned rings which support the tabla.

da द - A tabla bol of pakhawaj origin.

da ड - A tabla bol.

dadra दादरा - A semiclassical style of singing

dadra tal दादरा ताल - A common six beat tal used in light and semiclassical music.

dagga डग्गा - The large metal left hand drum.

dayan दायाँ - The small wooden right hand drum.

Delhi - See Dilli.

dhaa धा - A fundamental bol of both tabla and pakhawaj.

dhee धी - A fundamental bol.

dhi धि or धी - A fundamental bol.

dhin धिं or धीं - A fundamental bol.

dholak ढोलक - A crude folk drum characterized by a cylindrical wooden shell covered with skin on both sides.

dholak masala ढोलक मसाला - A paste applied to inner surface of left hand drum skin on many folk drums.

dholki ढोल्कि - A small folk drum popular in Maharashtra.

dhrupad ध्रुपद् - A classical style of music, once popular but today rare.

dhun धुन - 1) A light style of instrumental solo. 2) A musical religious chant.

di दि or दी - A tabla bol of pakhawaj origin.

Dilli दिल्ली - Delhi, the present capitol of India.

dilli baj दिल्ली बाज - The style of playing tabla, originally from Delhi, characterized by extensive use of the middle finger and strokes on the rim of the tabla.

din दिं - A bol of tabla and pakhawaj.

dipchandi tal दीपचंदी ताल - A common 14 beat tal.

drut द्रुत - 1) Fast tempo. 2) An archaic unit of time equal to two anudrut.

dugga - See dagga.

dugun दुगुन - A layakari of 2:1 (i.e., double time).

ektal एकताल - A common tal of 12 beats, however, non-standard versions may be found for 3, 4, 5, 7, and even 9 beats.

Farukhabad फरुखाबाद - 1) A town in northern Indian. 2) The gharana from this town.

filmi फ़िल्मी - 1) Pertaining to the film or movie industry. 2) A style of popular music.

gab गाब - The syahi.

ganda bandhan गंडा बन्धन - The ceremonial tying of thread around a new disciple's wrist signifying the beginning of ones discipleship.

gandharva veda गंधर्व वेद - The science of music.

gat गत - 1) A compositional type common in the Purbi style of playing. 2) The theme of an instrumental performance.

gatta गट्टा - The wooden dowels in the lacing.

gazal गजल - A style of poetic recitation, today a style of song.

ge गे - A bol for the left hand.

geet गीत - A song.

gha घ - A basic bol of the left hand.

gharana घराना - (Lit. "house") A particular subtradition or "school"

gharanedar घरानेदार - A representative of a particular gharana or school.

ghazal - see gazal.

ghe घे - A bol for the left hand.

ghi चि or घी - A bol for the left hand.

ghin घिं - A bol for the left hand.

gi गि or गी - A bol for the left hand.

gin गिं or गीं - A bol for the left hand.

girali गिरली - See chutta.

gittak गिट्टक - See gatta.

gudri गुडरी - The kundal.

Gujarat गुजरात - A state in northwest India.

guru bhai गरु भाइ - A fellow disciple under the teacher.

guru-shishya-parampara गुरु शिष्य परम्परा - The lineage of teacher to disciple.

harmonium हारमोनियम - A small hand-pumped reed-organ.

hathodi हथौड़ी - The small hammer used to tune the tabla.

hindustani sangeet हिंदुस्तानी संगीत - North Indian classical music.

jhala झाला - The fast rhythmic style of instrumental music characterized by a constant plucking of drone strings (chikari).

jhaptal झपताल - A common tal of 10 beats.

ka क - A tabla bol of the left hand.

kaherava tal कहरवा ताल - A common eight-beat tal.

kaida कायदा - A highly formalized approach to a tabla solo.

karnatic sangeet कर्नाटिक संगीत - See carnatic sangeet.

kat कत् - A tabla bol.

kathak कथक - A north Indian style of classical dance.

kawali कव्वाली - A style of Islamic devotional song.

kawali tal कव्वाली ताल - A tal of eight beats similar to kaherava.

kdan क्डां or क्डान् - A powerful bol of both pakhawaj and tabla.

ke के - A tabla bol of the left hand.

keherava - See kaherava.

kerva tal केरवा ताल - See kaherava, a common eight beat tal.

khali खाली - (Lit. "empty") Waved, opposite of bhari or tali.

khemta tal खेमटा ताल - A fairly common yet amorphous tal variously described as six or 12 beats.

khula खुला - (Lit. "open") Resonant strokes such as Ga, Toon, etc.

khula baj खुला बाज - (Lit. "open style") A style of tabla playing where the hands do not remain in contact with the drums, characteristic of the lucknowi style.

ki कि or की - A tabla bol of the left hand.

kinar किनार - (Lit. "edge") The chat.

kuri कूड़ी - The shell of the bayan.

laggi लग्गी - A fast lively style of playing, similar to rela, used in light styles of playing, particularly with bhajans, thumris, gazal, etc.

lahara लहरा - A simple, repetitive melody used to accompany tabla solos and kathak dance. Sometimes (incorrectly) referred to as naghma.

lakadi लकड़ी - (Lit. wood) The wooden shell of the tabla.

lakhnowi baj लखनवी बाज - The style of playing originating from Lucknow.

lav लव - 1) Maidan, sur, the part of the tabla's playing surface between the chat (kinar) and the syahi. 2) An archaic unit of time said to be equal to eight kshan.

lay लय - Tempo.

layakari लयकारी - 1) The relationship between the performed pulse of a composition and the theoretical beat. 2) Complex divisions of the beat.

lucknow लखनऊ - 1) A city in northern India. 2) The gharana from this area.

maidan मैदान - The main resonating membrane of tabla or pakhawaj.

manjira मञ्जीरा - Small cymbals.

matra मात्रा - The beat.

mira मीरा - A great woman saint.

mitti bayan मिट्टी बायां - A bayan made of clay.

mridang मृदंग or मृदङ्ग - Any two headed barrel shaped drum of the pakhawaj variety.

mridangam मृदंगम - A south Indian mridang.

mukhada मुखड़ा - A very small phrase or composition ending on sam. It may or may not have a tihai.

mukheda - See mukhada.

mundi मुंदी - A term use by Banarasi musicians to indicate khali.

na न - Fundamental tabla bol.

naa ना - Fundamental tabla bol.

nagada नगाड़ा - A pair of kettle drums played with sticks.

nal नाल - A dholki.

nrtya नृत्य - Dance.

padhant पढंत - The recitation of bols.

pakhawaj पखावज - A barrel shaped drum with playing heads on both sides.

pakhawaji पखावज्जी - One who plays the pakhawaj.

palla पल्ला - A section of the tihai that is repeated three times.

palta पलटा or पल्टा - A permutation of a kaida.

paran परण or परन - A class of small compositions derived from pakhawaj tradition.

paschami baj पश्चिमी बाज - The styles of dilli and ajrada gharanas.

peshkar पेशकार - (Lit. "introduction") An introductory movement similar to kaida but with a different system of permutation.

pital पीतल - (Lit. "brass") The brass shell of the bayan.

prakar प्रकार - Different varieties of theka.

prastar प्रस्तार - Permutations upon a kaida or given theme.

pudi पुड़ी - A tabla head.

Punjab पंजाब - 1) An area along the border between India and Pakistan. 2) The gharana from this area.

punjabi पंजाबी - (Lit. "from Punjab") A 16 beat tal similar to tintal.

Purbi पूरबी - (Lit. "Eastern") The style of playing in the Farukhabad, Lucknow, and Benares traditions.

ra र - A tabla bol.

ra ड़ - A tabla bol.

rassi रस्सी - The rope lacing on the dholak.

rela रेला - A very fast manipulation of small structures.

ri रि - A tabla bol.

riaz - See riyaz.

rupak tal रूपक ताल - A common seven beat tal with uncommon variations of 5, 6, 9 or 11 beats.

sam सम - The first beat of a cycle.

sangeet संगीत or सङ्गीत - Music and dance.

santoor - See santur.

santur संतुर - An Indian hammered dulcimer.

sarod सरोद - A stringed instrument similar to rabab.

shagird शागिर्द - A student or disciple.

shai शाई - Vernacular of syahi. See syahi.

shastriya sangeet शास्त्रीय संगीत - Classical music.

sidha सीधा - The small wooden right hand drum.

sitar सितार - A common long necked fretted instrument.

sitarkhani सितारखनी - A 16 beat tal which is the same as Punjabi theka.

ta ट - Fundamental tabla bol.

taa ता - Fundamental tabla bol of the right hand.

taali - See tali.

tabaliya तबलिया - A respectful term for a tabla player.

tabalji तब्बलजी - A slightly derogatory term for a tabla player.

tabla तबला - 1) The pair of Indian hand drums. 2) The right hand drum of the pair. 3) The Arabic word for any drum.

tabla tarang तबला तरंग - A musical instrument composed of numerous wooden tabla tuned to different pitches.

tal ताल - 1) The Indian system of rhythm. 2) A particular rhythmic cycle (e.g., tintal, rupak tal, etc.) 3) Clapping of hands. 4) (Archaic) A style of timekeeping in the marg sashabd kriya characterized by the striking of the stationary left hand with the right hand.

tal-lipi ताल-लिपि - Percussion notation.

tal paddhati ताल पद्धति - A theoretical framework of rhythm.

tali ताली - Clapped.

tanpura तानपूरा - A long necked, stringed instrument for providing the drone.

tasma तस्मा - The rawhide lacing of the tabla.

tat तत् - 1) A tabla bol. 2) A plucked string instrument (e.g., sitar, sarod, etc.)

tawaif तवाइफ़ - 1) A female entertainer. 2) A prostitute.

te ते or टे - A tabla bol.

tee ती - Fundamental tabla bol.

teental - See tintal.

theka ठेका - 1) The fundamental rhythmic pattern used for timekeeping. 2) A type of theme and variation, similar to peshkar, used by musicians of the Benares gharana.

thu थु or थू - A tabla bol.

thun थुं or थूं - A tabla bol.

ti ति or ती - Fundamental tabla bol.

tihai तिहाई - A cadenza composed of three identical sections.

tin तिं - Fundamental tabla bol.

tintal तीनताल - A very common tal of 16 beats.

too तु or तू - A tabla bol.

toon तुं or तूं - A tabla bol.

trital त्रिताल - Tintal, a common 16 beat tal.

tu तु - A tabla bol.

tun तुं - A tabla bol.

ustad उस्ताद - A learned man, a master.

vibhag विभाग - The measure or "bar"

QUICK REFERENCE
PAGE FOR BOLS

Dhaa (धा) - (Combination of *Taa* and *Ga*) standard technique 22, Purbi technique 60

Dha - TiTaGiRaNaGa (धा - तिट गिड़नाग) - (A common bol complex) technique 65

Dhee (धी) - (A basic bol with various techniques) technique similar to Dhin 36

Dhin (धिं) - (Combination of *Tin* and *Ga*) technique 24

Ga (ग) - (This is a common resonant stroke of the left hand) technique 21

Ge (गे) - (this is this is the same as *Ga*) technique 21

GiDaNaGa (गिड़नाग) - (Same as *GiRaNaGa*)

Gin (गिं) - (this is this is the same as *Ga*) technique 21

GiRaNaGa (गिड़नाग) - (a bol common in the Ajrada style of playing) technique 65

Ka (क) - (This is a common "slap" of the left hand) technique 19

Kat (कत्) - (A non-resonant stroke) technique 36

KiDaNaKa (किड़नाक) - (Same as *KiRaNaKa*)

KiRaNaKa (किड़नाक) - (A complex bol common in the Ajrada style of playing) technique 64

Kra (कृ) or (क्र) - (A flam) technique 37

Naa (ना) -(This is a common rim stroke) technique 20, used in tuning 14

Taa (ता) - (Semi-resonant stroke of the right hand), Dilli technique 22, Purbi technique 60

Ta - TiTaKiRaNaaKa (ता - तिट कि ड़नाक) - (A common bol) technique 64

Tee (ती) - (A nonresonant stroke of the right hand) technique 35

Tin (तिं) - (A resonant stroke of the right hand) technique 23

TiRaKiTa (तिरकिट) - (A basic bol complex of four strokes) Dilli technique 34, Purbi technique 61

TiRaKiTaTaKa (तिरकिट तक) - (A basic bol complex of six strokes) technique 62

TiTa (तिट) - (A basic bol complex of two strokes of the right hand) Dilli technique 33, Purbi technique 60

Too (तृ) - (A resonant stroke of the right hand) technique 35

Toon (तृ) - (same as Too) technique 35

ABOUT THE AUTHOR

David Courtney, Ph.D. was born in Houston, TX in 1953. He became interested in Indian music while he was still in high school. In 1971 he was host to a weekly program of classical Indian music on KPFT. He started to learn tabla in 1972. In January of 1974, he enrolled in the Ali Akbar College of Music and began studying pakhawaj under Ustad Zakir Hussain. It is from this period that his academic direction became firmly fixed toward Indian music. In 1976 while still only 22 he moved to Hyderabad to complete his training. He became a disciple of the late Ustad Shaik Dawood Khan of Hyderabad. In 1978 he married N. Chandrakantha, a well known vocalist in the Hyderabad area.

It was in 1980 that he moved back to the United States with his wife. Together they began teaching in the Houston area. Just months before returning, his first book was published. This book *Introduction to Tabla* was one of the few books written on tabla in the English language.

In the early 80's he was an early pioneer in the application of computers to traditional Indian music. This work on computers lead to his Doctoral Dissertation "A low Cost System for the Computerization of Indian Music" (1990 from IIAS - Greenwich University).

David Courtney is a prolific author on the subject of Indian Music. Aside from his first book, *Introduction to Tabla*, he has also co-authored *Elementary North Indian Vocal* and is full author for *Fundamentals of Tabla, Advanced Theory of Tabla* and *Manufacture and Repair of Tabla*. His articles have appeared in *Modern Drummer, Percussive Notes* and numerous other journals.

David Courtney is presently on the Board of Directors of the Texas Institute for Indian Studies. He is also an active artist with Young Audiences. He has made countless performances around the world, made numerous recordings, and has performed on stage, radio, TV and Disk on countless occasions. In 1996 he was given (along with his wife, Chandrakantha) the "Award of Excellence" by the American Telugu Association for his artistic contributions in the field of music.

Chandrakantha Courtney performed the vocal, sitar, harmonium and the tanpura on the accompanying audio recording. She is well known in the Indian community both in the United States and Asia. She was formerly an artist in All India Radio of Vijaywada and Hyderabad. She has performed music for several films, disks, cassettes, and countless radio and TV performances. She has performed extensively in India, South Africa, Malaysia, Singapore, Germany and the U.S. With her husband, David Courtney, she travels throughout the U.S. and Asia teaching and performing. She is an artist with Young Audiences, and on the Board of Directors of the Texas Institute for Indian Studies. She is the co-author of a book *Elementary North Indian Vocal*. She was awarded "Artist of the Year" by *Asian Women*, and along with her husband she was given an award of recognition for outstanding contributions to the arts by the American Telugu Association.

CONTACT INFO
David & Chandrakantha Courtney
box 270685
Houston, TX 77005
USA
(713) 665 0186 (fax)
david@chandrakantha.com (e-mail)

Visit
David and Chandrakantha Courtney's Homepage
http://chandrakantha.com/